The Nuclear Regulatory Commission

The Nuclear Regulatory Commission

Fred Clement

CHELSEA HOUSE PUBLISHERS

On the cover: Oregon's Trojan nuclear power plant.

Chelsea House Publishers
Editor-in-Chief: Nancy Toff
Executive Editor: Remmel T. Nunn
Managing Editor: Karyn Gullen Browne
Copy Chief: Juliann Barbato
Picture Editor: Adrian G. Allen
Art Director: Maria Epes
Manufacturing Manager: Gerald Levine

Know Your Government
Senior Editor: Kathy Kuhtz

Staff for THE NUCLEAR REGULATORY COMMISSION
Assistant Editor: Gillian Bucky
Deputy Copy Chief: Ellen Scordato
Editorial Assistant: Theodore Keyes
Picture Researcher: Dixon and Turner Research Associates
Assistant Art Director: Laurie Jewell
Designer: Noreen M. Lamb
Production Coordinator: Joseph Romano

First Printing

1 3 5 7 9 8 6 4 2

Library of Congress Cataloging-in-Publication Data

Clement, Fred.
  The Nuclear Regulatory Commission.

  (Know your government)
  Bibliography: p.
  Includes index.
  Summary: Surveys the history of the Nuclear Regulatory Commission, with descriptions of its structure, current function, and influence on American society.
  1. U.S. Nuclear Regulatory Commission—Juvenile literature. [1. U.S. Nuclear Regulatory Commission] I. Title. II. Series: Know your government (New York, N.Y.) TK9152.C54   1989   353.0087'22   88-18154

ISBN 1-55546-129-8

CONTENTS

Introduction 7

1 The Guardian of Nuclear Power 15

2 Atoms for Peace 21

3 Coming of Age 41

4 Regulating Nuclear Power 57

   Feature Nuclear Power: How a Reactor Works 62

5 Beyond Nuclear Power Plant Licensing 77

6 The NRC Tomorrow 89

   Organizational Chart The Nuclear Regulatory

   Commission 92

Glossary 93

Selected References 95

Index 97

KNOW YOUR GOVERNMENT

THE AMERICAN RED CROSS

THE BUREAU OF INDIAN AFFAIRS

THE CENTRAL INTELLIGENCE AGENCY

THE COMMISSION ON CIVIL RIGHTS

THE DEPARTMENT OF AGRICULTURE

THE DEPARTMENT OF THE AIR FORCE

THE DEPARTMENT OF THE ARMY

THE DEPARTMENT OF COMMERCE

THE DEPARTMENT OF DEFENSE

THE DEPARTMENT OF EDUCATION

THE DEPARTMENT OF ENERGY

THE DEPARTMENT OF HEALTH AND HUMAN SERVICES

THE DEPARTMENT OF HOUSING AND URBAN DEVELOPMENT

THE DEPARTMENT OF THE INTERIOR

THE DEPARTMENT OF JUSTICE

THE DEPARTMENT OF LABOR

THE DEPARTMENT OF THE NAVY

THE DEPARTMENT OF STATE

THE DEPARTMENT OF TRANSPORTATION

THE DEPARTMENT OF THE TREASURY

THE DRUG ENFORCEMENT ADMINISTRATION

THE ENVIRONMENTAL PROTECTION AGENCY

THE EQUAL EMPLOYMENT OPPORTUNITIES COMMISSION

THE FEDERAL AVIATION ADMINISTRATION

THE FEDERAL BUREAU OF INVESTIGATION

THE FEDERAL COMMUNICATIONS COMMISSION

THE FEDERAL GOVERNMENT: HOW IT WORKS

THE FEDERAL RESERVE SYSTEM

THE FEDERAL TRADE COMMISSION

THE FOOD AND DRUG ADMINISTRATION

THE FOREST SERVICE

THE HOUSE OF REPRESENTATIVES

THE IMMIGRATION AND NATURALIZATION SERVICE

THE INTERNAL REVENUE SERVICE

THE LIBRARY OF CONGRESS

THE NATIONAL AERONAUTICS AND SPACE ADMINISTRATION

THE NATIONAL ARCHIVES AND RECORDS ADMINISTRATION

THE NATIONAL FOUNDATION ON THE ARTS AND HUMANITIES

THE NATIONAL PARK SERVICE

THE NATIONAL SCIENCE FOUNDATION

THE NUCLEAR REGULATORY COMMISSION

THE PEACE CORPS

THE PRESIDENCY

THE PUBLIC HEALTH SERVICE

THE SECURITIES AND EXCHANGE COMMISSION

THE SENATE

THE SMALL BUSINESS ADMINISTRATION

THE SMITHSONIAN

THE SUPREME COURT

THE TENNESSEE VALLEY AUTHORITY

THE U.S. ARMS CONTROL AND DISARMAMENT AGENCY

THE U.S. COAST GUARD

THE U.S. CONSTITUTION

THE U.S. FISH AND WILDLIFE SERVICE

THE U.S. INFORMATION AGENCY

THE U.S. MARINE CORPS

THE U.S. MINT

THE U.S. POSTAL SERVICE

THE U.S. SECRET SERVICE

THE VETERANS ADMINISTRATION

CHELSEA HOUSE PUBLISHERS

Government: Crises of Confidence

Arthur M. Schlesinger, jr.

From the start, Americans have regarded their government with a mixture of reliance and mistrust. The men who founded the republic did not doubt the indispensability of government. "If men were angels," observed the 51st Federalist Paper, "no government would be necessary." But men are not angels. Because human beings are subject to wicked as well as to noble impulses, government was deemed essential to assure freedom and order.

At the same time, the American revolutionaries knew that government could also become a source of injury and oppression. The men who gathered in Philadelphia in 1787 to write the Constitution therefore had two purposes in mind. They wanted to establish a strong central authority and to limit that central authority's capacity to abuse its power.

To prevent the abuse of power, the Founding Fathers wrote two basic principles into the new Constitution. The principle of federalism divided power between the state governments and the central authority. The principle of the separation of powers subdivided the central authority itself into three branches—the executive, the legislative, and the judiciary—so that "each may be a check on the other." The *Know Your Government* series focuses on the major executive departments and agencies in these branches of the federal government.

The Constitution did not plan the executive branch in any detail. After vesting the executive power in the president, it assumed the existence of "executive departments" without specifying what these departments should be. Congress began defining their functions in 1789 by creating the Departments of State, Treasury, and War. The secretaries in charge of these departments made up President Washington's first cabinet. Congress also provided for a legal officer, and President Washington soon invited the attorney general, as he was called, to attend cabinet meetings. As need required, Congress created more executive departments.

Setting up the cabinet was only the first step in organizing the American state. With almost no guidance from the Constitution, President Washington, seconded by Alexander Hamilton, his brilliant secretary of the treasury, equipped the infant republic with a working administrative structure. The Federalists believed in both executive energy and executive accountability and set high standards for public appointments. The Jeffersonian opposition had less faith in strong government and preferred local government to the central authority. But when Jefferson himself became president in 1801, although he set out to change the direction of policy, he found no reason to alter the framework the Federalists had erected.

By 1801 there were about 3,000 federal civilian employees in a nation of a little more than 5 million people. Growth in territory and population steadily enlarged national responsibilities. Thirty years later, when Jackson was president, there were more than 11,000 government workers in a nation of 13 million. The federal establishment was increasing at a faster rate than the population.

Jackson's presidency brought significant changes in the federal service. He believed that the executive branch contained too many officials who saw their jobs as "species of property" and as "a means of promoting individual interest." Against the idea of a permanent service based on life tenure, Jackson argued for the periodic redistribution of federal offices, contending that this was the democratic way and that official duties could be made "so plain and simple that men of intelligence may readily qualify themselves for their performance." He called this policy rotation-in-office. His opponents called it the spoils system.

In fact, partisan legend exaggerated the extent of Jackson's removals. More than 80 percent of federal officeholders retained their jobs. Jackson discharged no larger a proportion of government workers than Jefferson had done a generation earlier. But the rise in these years of mass political parties gave federal patronage new importance as a means of building the party and of rewarding activists. Jackson's successors were less restrained in the distribu-

tion of spoils. As the federal establishment grew—to nearly 40,000 by 1861—
the politicization of the public service excited increasing concern.

After the Civil War the spoils system became a major political issue.
High-minded men condemned it as the root of all political evil. The spoilsmen,
said the British commentator James Bryce, "have distorted and depraved the
mechanism of politics." Patronage, by giving jobs to unqualified, incompetent,
and dishonest persons, lowered the standards of public service and nourished
corrupt political machines. Office-seekers pursued presidents and cabinet
secretaries without mercy. "Patronage," said Ulysses S. Grant after his
presidency, "is the bane of the presidential office." "Every time I appoint
someone to office," said another political leader, "I make a hundred enemies
and one ingrate." George William Curtis, the president of the National Civil
Service Reform League, summed up the indictment. He said,

> The theory which perverts public trusts into party spoils, making public
> employment dependent upon personal favor and not on proved merit,
> necessarily ruins the self-respect of public employees, destroys the
> function of party in a republic, prostitutes elections into a desperate
> strife for personal profit, and degrades the national character by lower-
> ing the moral tone and standard of the country.

The object of civil service reform was to promote efficiency and honesty in
the public service and to bring about the ethical regeneration of public life. Over
bitter opposition from politicians, the reformers in 1883 passed the Pendleton
Act, establishing a bipartisan Civil Service Commission, competitive examinations, and appointment on merit. The Pendleton Act also gave the president
authority to extend by executive order the number of "classified" jobs—that is,
jobs subject to the merit system. The act applied initially only to about 14,000
of the more than 100,000 federal positions. But by the end of the 19th century
40 percent of federal jobs had moved into the classified category.

Civil service reform was in part a response to the growing complexity of
American life. As society grew more organized and problems more technical,
official duties were no longer so plain and simple that any person of intelligence
could perform them. In public service, as in other areas, the all-round man was
yielding ground to the expert, the amateur to the professional. The excesses
of the spoils system thus provoked the counter-ideal of scientific public administration, separate from politics and, as far as possible, insulated against it.

The cult of the expert, however, had its own excesses. The idea that
administration could be divorced from policy was an illusion. And in the realm
of policy, the expert, however much segregated from partisan politics, can

never attain perfect objectivity. He remains the prisoner of his own set of values. It is these values rather than technical expertise that determine fundamental judgments of public policy. To turn over such judgments to experts, moreover, would be to abandon democracy itself; for in a democracy final decisions must be made by the people and their elected representatives. "The business of the expert," the British political scientist Harold Laski rightly said, "is to be on tap and not on top."

Politics, however, were deeply ingrained in American folkways. This meant intermittent tension between the presidential government, elected every four years by the people, and the permanent government, which saw presidents come and go while it went on forever. Sometimes the permanent government knew better than its political masters; sometimes it opposed or sabotaged valuable new initiatives. In the end a strong president with effective cabinet secretaries could make the permanent government responsive to presidential purpose, but it was often an exasperating struggle.

The struggle within the executive branch was less important, however, than the growing impatience with bureaucracy in society as a whole. The 20th century saw a considerable expansion of the federal establishment. The Great Depression and the New Deal led the national government to take on a variety of new responsibilities. The New Deal extended the federal regulatory apparatus. By 1940, in a nation of 130 million people, the number of federal workers for the first time passed the 1 million mark. The Second World War brought federal civilian employment to 3.8 million in 1945. With peace, the federal establishment declined to around 2 million by 1950. Then growth resumed, reaching 2.8 million by the 1980s.

The New Deal years saw rising criticism of "big government" and "bureau-cracy." Businessmen resented federal regulation. Conservatives worried about the impact of paternalistic government on individual self-reliance, on community responsibility, and on economic and personal freedom. The nation in effect renewed the old debate between Hamilton and Jefferson in the early republic, although with an ironic exchange of positions. For the Hamiltonian constituency, the "rich and well-born," once the advocate of affirmative government, now condemned government intervention, while the Jeffersonian constituency, the plain people, once the advocate of a weak central government and of states' rights, now favored government intervention.

In the 1980s, with the presidency of Ronald Reagan, the debate has burst out with unusual intensity. According to conservatives, government interven-tion abridges liberty, stifles enterprise, and is inefficient, wasteful, and arbitrary. It disturbs the harmony of the self-adjusting market and creates worse troubles than it solves. Get government off our backs, according to the popular cliché, and our problems will solve themselves. When government is necessary, let it be at the local level, close to the people. Above all, stop the inexorable growth of the federal government.

In fact, for all the talk about the "swollen" and "bloated" bureaucracy, the federal establishment has not been growing as inexorably as many Americans seem to believe. In 1949, it consisted of 2.1 million people. Thirty years later, while the country had grown by 70 million, the federal force had grown only by 750,000. Federal workers were a smaller percentage of the population in 1985 than they were in 1955—or in 1940. The federal establishment, in short, has not kept pace with population growth. Moreover, national defense and the postal service account for 60 percent of federal employment.

Why then the widespread idea about the remorseless growth of government? It is partly because in the 1960s the national government assumed new and intrusive functions: affirmative action in civil rights, environmental protection, safety and health in the workplace, community organization, legal aid to the poor. Although this enlargement of the federal regulatory role was accompanied by marked growth in the size of government on all levels, the expansion has taken place primarily in state and local government. Whereas the federal force increased by only 27 percent in the 30 years after 1950, the state and local government force increased by an astonishing 212 percent.

Despite the statistics, the conviction flourishes in some minds that the national government is a steadily growing behemoth swallowing up the liberties of the people. The foes of Washington prefer local government, feeling it is closer to the people and therefore allegedly more responsive to popular needs. Obviously there is a great deal to be said for settling local questions locally. But local government is characteristically the government of the locally powerful. Historically, the way the locally powerless have won their human and constitutional rights has often been through appeal to the national government. The national government has vindicated racial justice against local bigotry, defended the Bill of Rights against local vigilantism, and protected natural resources against local greed. It has civilized industry and secured the rights of labor organizations. Had the states' rights creed prevailed, there would perhaps still be slavery in the United States.

The national authority, far from diminishing the individual, has given most Americans more personal dignity and liberty than ever before. The individual freedoms destroyed by the increase in national authority have been in the main the freedom to deny black Americans their rights as citizens; the freedom to put small children to work in mills and immigrants in sweatshops; the freedom to pay starvation wages, require barbarous working hours, and permit squalid working conditions; the freedom to deceive in the sale of goods and securities; the freedom to pollute the environment—all freedoms that, one supposes, a civilized nation can readily do without.

"Statements are made," said President John F. Kennedy in 1963, "labelling the Federal Government an outsider, an intruder, an adversary. . . . The United States Government is not a stranger or not an enemy. It is the people of fifty states joining in a national effort. . . . Only a great national effort by a great people working together can explore the mysteries of space, harvest the products at the bottom of the ocean, and mobilize the human, natural, and material resources of our lands."

So an old debate continues. However, Americans are of two minds. When pollsters ask large, spacious questions—Do you think government has become too involved in your lives? Do you think government should stop regulating business?—a sizable majority opposes big government. But when asked specific questions about the practical work of government—Do you favor social security? unemployment compensation? Medicare? health and safety standards in factories? environmental protection? government guarantee of jobs for everyone seeking employment? price and wage controls when inflation threatens?—a sizable majority approves of intervention.

In general, Americans do not want less government. What they want is more efficient government. They want government to do a better job. For a time in the 1970s, with Vietnam and Watergate, Americans lost confidence in the national government. In 1964, more than three-quarters of those polled had thought the national government could be trusted to do right most of the time. By 1980 only one-quarter was prepared to offer such trust. But by 1984 trust in the federal government to manage national affairs had climbed back to 45 percent.

Bureaucracy is a term of abuse. But it is impossible to run any large organization, whether public or private, without a bureaucracy's division of labor and hierarchy of authority. And we live in a world of large organizations. Without bureaucracy modern society would collapse. The problem is not to abolish bureaucracy, but to make it flexible, efficient, and capable of innovation.

Two hundred years after the drafting of the Constitution, Americans still regard government with a mixture of reliance and mistrust—a good combination. Mistrust is the best way to keep government reliable. Informed criticism is the means of correcting governmental inefficiency, incompetence, and arbitrariness; that is, of best enabling government to play its essential role. For without government, we cannot attain the goals of the Founding Fathers. Without an understanding of government, we cannot have the informed criticism that makes government do the job right. It is the duty of every American citizen to know our government—which is what this series is all about.

An atom-bomb cloud billows over the Bikini Islands in the South Pacific. The United States used the islands as a test site for its atomic weapons program in 1946 and 1954.

ONE

The Guardian of Nuclear Power

Since the 1960s, nuclear power plants have filled a significant portion of the nation's electricity demands. In 1987, 15 percent of the electrical energy consumed by U.S. homes and factories was produced by nuclear power plants. At the same time, the use of nuclear technology by the medical community has reached new heights, helping to treat cancers such as Hodgkin's disease and diagnose illnesses from heart attacks to brain tumors. Universities and industries have also contributed to the nation's health and growth by harnessing nuclear energy. Yet handling nuclear material even for peaceful purposes can be dangerous, if not deadly. Unsafe construction or operation of a nuclear power plant can be disastrous. For this reason, the Nuclear Regulatory Commission (NRC) plays a vital role in safeguarding American citizens and their environment from the dangers inherent in this valuable resource. The NRC serves as the nation's watchdog over peaceful uses of nuclear energy, preserving the health and safety of people, protecting the fish and wildlife of their environment, and promoting the security of the nation.

Despite this heavy responsibility, the NRC is one of the younger federal agencies. Perhaps this is not surprising, as nuclear technology itself is relatively new. The NRC was established in 1974, when its predecessor, the Atomic Energy Commission (AEC), disbanded. Since 1946, the AEC had worn two hats; it was responsible for nurturing the growth of the nuclear industry and for protecting public safety and the environment from the dangers of nuclear energy. By the early 1970s, when the nation perceived the Atomic Energy Commission as failing to do either job adequately, Congress dismantled the agency and created in its place two separate organizations—the Energy Research and Development Administration, which inherited responsibility for promoting the growth of the nuclear industry, and the NRC, which was given regulatory duties such as governing the safe construction and operation of nuclear facilities.

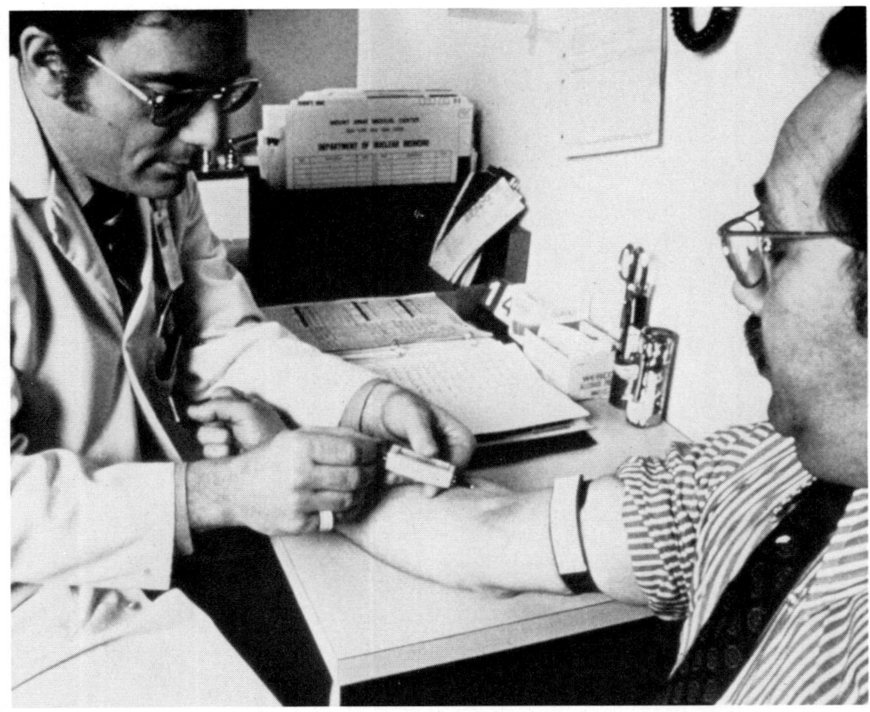

A doctor treats his patient with nuclear chemicals. The medical advances made possible by nuclear technology have enabled physicians to diagnose and treat previously disabling and fatal illnesses.

Today, the NRC is constantly at work, inspecting the nation's nuclear power plants, supervising transportation of nuclear materials on railroads and highways, responding swiftly to nuclear accidents, and watching over the thriving nuclear medicine industry and academic research. In short, the NRC is on guard for any telltale sign of mishap and working to prevent the occurrence of accidents.

When accidents do happen, however, the NRC takes center stage. When a nuclear plant located at Three Mile Island in Pennsylvania malfunctioned on March 28, 1979, the NRC arrived to help minimize damage, prevent further harm from occurring, and evaluate the event to avert similar problems in the future.

Despite the great advances made possible by nuclear technology, the tension that destroyed the Atomic Energy Commission—between nuclear development, which propels the nuclear industry forward, and regulation, which reins in this growth in an effort to ensure the safety of each nuclear facility—is still a force with which the NRC must contend. Because nuclear energy is a relatively young phenomenon (the first nuclear-generated electricity was not produced until 1951), the industry is still undergoing growing pains and public acceptance is mixed. Although many people may acknowledge the need for inexpensive electric power, for example, they still question technology that allows a deadly explosion like that at the Soviet Union's Chernobyl nuclear power plant in 1986. While admitting that nuclear power may be one answer to the question, "What do we do for electricity when the world's oil supplies run out?," at the same time they wonder how best to control the steady buildup of harmful waste from nuclear plants. And although the public realizes that nuclear power is here to stay, it cringes at the specter of radiation-caused disease, a poisoned environment, and the horror of a nuclear disaster.

Resolving these questions safely and satisfactorily is the full-time job of more than 3,200 people at the NRC's headquarters in Maryland and at regional offices across the nation. Through its work in licensing the operation of nuclear reactors, guiding research toward ever-more-secure plant construction materials, helping state governments to oversee safer nuclear programs, and forming prudent rules and enforcing adherence to them, the NRC protects the nation, its people, and its lands. At the same time, the agency facilitates the cautious, reliable application of nuclear power.

Nuclear technology was first developed in the United States for the purposes of warfare. As physicist J. Robert Oppenheimer watched the first atomic bomb cloud mushroom to the heavens in a test explosion on July 16, 1945, a passage

*Physicist J. Robert Oppenheimer directed the nuclear weap-
ons research group that built the first atomic bombs during
World War II. He later became a vocal advocate of civilian and
international control of atomic energy.*

from the Hindu holy text the *Bhagavad-Gita* flashed through his mind: "I am become Death, the shatterer of worlds." Soon thereafter, when the U.S. Army Air Corps dropped atomic bombs on Hiroshima and Nagasaki in Japan—clinching the end of World War II—the power of nuclear energy to shatter worlds was unalterably etched on the human consciousness. Protecting the United States and its citizens from such dangers, and at the same time allowing for the safe, peaceful use of nuclear energy, is the responsibility of the Nuclear Regulatory Commission.

In 1951, at the AEC's national reactor testing center in Arco, Idaho, this light bulb demonstrated the first electricity generated by nuclear heat. This landmark event sparked interest in the development of nuclear energy for commercial purposes.

TWO

Atoms for Peace

Nuclear technology was in its infancy in the early 1940s, when scientists in the United States first harnessed enough nuclear energy to detonate an atomic bomb. Soon after the United States entered World War II in 1941, the government instituted a nuclear weapons program under the auspices of the United States Army. Called the Manhattan Engineer District (or simply the Manhattan Project) to disguise its activities, the program began intensive research into nuclear technology and, on July 16, 1945, tested its first atomic bomb at a deserted site in New Mexico.

A month later, the United States dropped atomic bombs on the Japanese cities of Hiroshima and Nagasaki, hastening the end of World War II and ushering in the nuclear age. At the same time, the nation established a world monopoly on the power of the atom. Although it would lose that monopoly over the next three decades, the United States would take a leading role in harnessing the atom for medicine, science, electric power, and other peaceful purposes.

At the end of the war, President Harry S. Truman introduced legislation to transfer nuclear research to civilian control, and in 1946 Congress established the Atomic Energy Commission through passage of the Atomic Energy Act. With an eye toward protecting the nation's atomic weapons monopoly and advancing nuclear technology, Congress gave the AEC sweeping authority.

The horrible destructive potential of nuclear energy is starkly depicted in this photograph of the aftermath of the bombing of Nagasaki, Japan, by the United States in 1945.

What once had been the bailiwick of the military now became the AEC's domain: the production of nuclear fuels and atomic weapons for military needs and the concomitant research and development programs. From the Manhattan Project, the group that developed the nuclear weapons used in World War II, the AEC inherited facilities, personnel, and classified data.

To direct the use of nuclear energy in the United States, five civilians—lawyers and administrators in nuclear industry—were named Atomic Energy Commissioners by the president and confirmed by the Senate. One of the commissioners, David E. Lilienthal, was named chairman of the AEC. During the war, Lilienthal had been chairman of the Tennessee Valley Authority, developers of a system of dams that had supplied the power for an atomic plant at Oak Ridge, Tennessee, which had in turn prepared uranium—a nuclear fuel—for the Manhattan Project.

"In the whole of history," wrote Lilienthal in his 1963 book *Change, Hope and the Bomb*, "no single force has cast a greater terror over all mankind than the Atom." To ensure trouble-free development of this new and potentially dangerous technology, Congress assigned regulatory duties to the AEC. At the time, this marriage of development and safety regulation seemed sensible because one serious nuclear accident could devastate the program. However, as time went by, the defects of this policy would become apparent.

In the early years, while the marriage was still secure, scientists unlocked nuclear mysteries under the AEC's watchful eye. In December 1951, at the AEC's reactor-testing center in Arco, Idaho, technicians generated the first electrical power from a nuclear reactor. This new use of atomic power represented a turning point in nuclear development. After considering the concept of nuclear power, the manufacturers of power plants and electrical utilities concluded that, given time, nuclear plants could generate electricity financially competitive with that produced by oil, coal, or other conventional fuel sources.

David E. Lilienthal, the first chairman of the Atomic Energy Commission. Lilienthal and four other commissioners were charged with promoting and regulating the development of nuclear energy in the United States.

Construction workers put the finishing touches on a dam built under the auspices of the Tennessee Valley Authority. Created by Congress in 1933 to foster development of the Tennessee River basin, the TVA oversaw a series of dams that produced hydroelectric power for the surrounding area.

The AEC's national reactor testing center in Arco, Idaho, where electricity was first generated by nuclear energy in 1951. The site is now a national historic landmark.

Despite the novelty of this concept, AEC chairman Gordon Dean—who had replaced Lilienthal in 1950—was convinced of its potential. In the spring of 1953 Dean urged the government to encourage development of nuclear power for commercial purposes—a suggestion that dramatically opposed AEC policy, which prohibited nongovernment ownership of nuclear reactors and fuel.

Since the end of World War II, the U.S. government had sole ownership of the materials used to produce nuclear fission (atomic reactions), as spelled out in the Atomic Energy Act of 1946. At that time, atomic power meant only one thing: the atomic bomb. The thought of that generated fear. Given the awesome destructive power of the atomic bomb, it was in the best interests of the nation's security to restrict atomic knowledge and materials. Not surprisingly, the government also owned the facilities that produced and used nuclear material. Thus, Dean's recommendation—that nongovernment entities be allowed to own nuclear reactors and share atomic technology—represented a dramatic policy shift. Going a step further, Dean also proposed that these companies be allowed to own or lease fissionable materials. In essence, he wanted to see them become the suppliers and makers of nuclear reactors and nuclear power and in so doing foster a national nuclear industry for peaceful

Gordon Dean became chairman of the AEC in 1950. Under his leadership, the agency guided nuclear energy into the commercial sphere.

purposes. For that to happen, Dean realized, the government would have to share its nuclear materials and technological information and include industries in designing and engineering reactors.

The idea of private nuclear development gained an added impetus when the Soviet Union tested its first thermonuclear bomb (a device in which an explosion is caused by the *fusion* of atomic particles, rather than the *fission*, or splitting, reaction found in previous nuclear weapons). To the United States, this event not only signaled the end of its lone membership in the "nuclear club" but also stimulated thinking behind a program of peaceful uses of atomic energy as opposed to military applications. This philosophy held that development of peaceful uses of the atom could benefit the United States and its friends and, by spreading peace, help curb war.

In December 1953, President Dwight D. Eisenhower announced to the world his plans for advancing nuclear technology. Addressing the United Nations, in what became known as his "Atoms for Peace" speech, Eisenhower

President Dwight D. Eisenhower (right) and U.S. postmaster general Arthur Summerfield (center) display a sheet of three-cent stamps issued to commemorate the president's "Atoms for Peace" program in 1955. The stamps feature twin globes encircled by atomic rings, symbolizing Eisenhower's hope for worldwide cooperation in developing atomic power for peaceful uses.

proposed initiatives for peaceful uses of atomic power. He anticipated applying "atomic energy to the needs of agriculture, medicine, and other peaceful activities. A special purpose would be to provide abundant electrical energy in the power-starved areas of the world."

In his budget message to Congress the following month, Eisenhower recommended amending the 1946 Atomic Energy Act in line with Gordon Dean's suggestions. Namely, the president proposed sharing information as well as fissionable materials and nuclear power with friendly nations. Later that year, Congress passed the Atomic Energy Act of 1954. Like its 1946 predecessor, this law also linked regulation with development under the AEC's umbrella, requiring the commission to license facilities and operators producing or using radioactive materials. In the case of nuclear power plants, the legislation required a two-phase licensing process: a license first to build, followed by a license later to operate the reactor. Furthermore, the law permitted licensed private companies to own and use nuclear facilities, liberalized patent rights, and enhanced access to technical data. In short, it introduced development of nuclear energy into private industry.

The infant nuclear industry grew rapidly. In 1957, construction ended on the nation's first commercially operating nuclear power plant, located in Shippingport, Pennsylvania. A joint project of the AEC and the Duquesne Light Company, the plant was a 60 MWe (megawatts of electric power) facility. Almost immediately thereafter, Westinghouse, one of the two major nuclear equipment manufacturers (General Electric was the other), contracted with an association of New England utility companies and the AEC to build an even more advanced plant than the one at Shippingport. Located in Rowe, Massachusetts, the "Yankee" plant boasted a 185 MWe reactor.

The booming nuclear industry received a sudden jolt in 1957, with the publication of a major AEC safety study, entitled "Theoretical Possibilities and Consequences of Major Accidents in Large Nuclear Power Plants." The study showed that thousands of residents might be killed or injured up to 75 miles from a major nuclear reactor accident, while property damage could reach $7 billion. The nuclear industry worried that this potential for catastrophe would frighten away major financial investment in large-scale nuclear reactor development. The threat of bankruptcy, the inability to obtain insurance, and other concerns were overwhelming. But investment did not dry up and the nuclear industry's growth did not stop because at that point Congress stepped in and passed the Price-Anderson amendment to the 1954 Atomic Energy Act. In effect, the federal government underwrote the financial responsibility of utility companies and manufacturers of nuclear reactor equipment in the event of a

Glenn T. Seaborg was a major figure in nuclear research before he was named chairman of the AEC in 1961. During his 10-year term as head of the AEC, Seaborg, codiscoverer of plutonium and recipient of the Nobel Prize for chemistry in 1951, saw nuclear industry come under increasing attack from environmental and public-interest groups.

nuclear reactor disaster. From that point on, the industry moved ahead briskly.

Helping in this growth was University of California chemist Glenn T. Seaborg, who, at age 49, was named AEC chairman in 1961. The son of a machinist in Ishpeming, a small mining town in northwestern Michigan, Seaborg was 10 years old when his family moved to California. He graduated Phi Beta Kappa with a degree in chemistry from the University of California at Los Angeles, and later earned a Ph.D. from the University of California at Berkeley. In 1940, Seaborg's work led to the discovery of plutonium, a material that could be used to fuel nuclear reactors and weapons. During World War II, Seaborg led a Manhattan Project group that isolated enough pure plutonium to build the atomic bomb. His pioneering work on plutonium won Seaborg and University of California physics professor Edwin M. McMillan the Nobel Prize in 1951. Before being named AEC chairman, Seaborg had also served as director of nuclear chemical research at Berkeley's Lawrence Radiation Laboratory and had become chancellor of the university.

Construction began on New Jersey's Oyster Creek nuclear power plant in 1963. Nuclear development boomed after the Oyster Creek plant demonstrated that nuclear power could be financially competitive with power generated from conventional fuels.

Committed to development of the nuclear industry, Seaborg set his sights accordingly, and by 1963 the industry passed a major milestone. Jersey Central Power and Light Company announced it was buying a 640 MWe nuclear reactor from General Electric Company for its Oyster Creek, New Jersey, power plant. For the first time, a nuclear power plant would be built that was able to supply electricity as inexpensively as fossil fuels (coal, gas, and oil) could. Had nuclear fuel costs been significantly higher, the budding nuclear industry would have been less appealing to profit-conscious investors in nuclear power. On average, however, the cost of fissionable materials was significantly lower than that of fossil fuels.

Nuclear reactors were soon in great demand. Between 1962 and 1965, construction permit applications for some 11 units streamed into the AEC, followed by 15 more in 1966. In those five years, the average size of a reactor more than doubled, from 325 to 780 MWe. By 1967, reactor capacity had risen to 850 MWe. The nuclear industry had become big business.

Then, several social and economic factors combined to slow this growth. One of the chief causes of this slowdown was a growing awareness of the danger to public health, public safety, ecology, and environmental quality in the areas surrounding existing nuclear plants. Increasingly, public-interest groups and environmentalists began to challenge the nuclear industry over such dangers as "thermal pollution," caused by the release of heated water from a nuclear plant into a river or lake. Typically, a plant took in cool water upstream, used it to carry off excess heat produced in the reactor, and then released the heated water downstream. (Less than one-third of the heat generated in a nuclear plant could be converted into electricity, as compared to about two-fifths for a fossil-fuel plant.) However, this cooling process raised the temperature of the downstream river and changed the river's nature and ecology, at times destructively. The warmed water killed some fish species, fostered the development of new ones, and promoted algae and other forms of fast-growing vegetation. Environmentalists demanded that nuclear plants not be allowed to continue operation unless they came up with a plan to counteract such negative effects on the environment.

Likewise, radiation hazards came under more intense scrutiny by the end of the 1960s. Following reports of higher infant death rates near nuclear plants, John W. Gofman and Arthur R. Tamplin of the AEC's Lawrence Radiation Laboratory in Livermore, California, conducted an investigation and concluded that radioactive particles released by nuclear plants into the atmosphere could harm infants and fetuses. Gofman, a medical physicist, physician, and codiscoverer of four radioisotopes (radioactive forms of chemical elements), was an

Workers examine fish for signs of radioactive contamination in waters near a nuclear power plant in Washington. Nuclear power came under fire by the end of the 1960s as environmentalists and public-interest groups charged that the industry posed a hazard to the environment and to public health.

associate director of Lawrence's Biomedical Research Division in 1969. Tamplin, who had a Ph.D. in biophysics, served as a group leader in Gofman's division. Together, the two charged that the AEC's standards of "safe" radiation exposure levels were too high. They determined that to prevent thousands of deaths from cancer each year, the AEC's "acceptable" levels should be reduced to one-tenth or less of the figure then in use.

In 1971, antinuclear groups targeted a third problem, the emergency core-cooling system (ECCS). In the event of an accident, a reactor's power can be lowered by means of control rods (made of a material that absorbs neutrons, which sustain atomic reactions) inserted into the reactor's core. The heat of radioactive decay cannot be stopped, however, and the ECCS is used to absorb this heat and prevent the fuel rods from melting. In the absence of an ECCS, a reactor core could potentially overheat to about 5,000 degrees and then melt through everything under it, including the earth. (This eventuality is known as the "China Syndrome," named for the country where the reactor hypothetically would emerge if it melted through the center of the earth. In fact, after sinking several feet into the ground, the molten metal would be cooled enough to stop melting.) In a report released in May 1971, the AEC questioned the adequacy of the ECCS. With that report, antinuclear groups brought into question the basic safety of nuclear reactors in an accident situation.

Nuclear waste disposal became an increasingly bothersome issue as well because of the threat it posed to public and environmental health. Capable of causing cancer, birth defects, and other afflictions, radioactive waste—the debris left over from nuclear reactions—had been accumulating since the 1940s. Because many radioactive elements remain dangerous for thousands of years, the nuclear industry warehoused waste as securely as possible in areas where it could cause the least harm. For instance, the industry stored liquid waste from reactors in stainless steel tanks encased in concrete in three locations—near Idaho Falls, Idaho; in Aiken, South Carolina; and in Richland, Washington. However, according to a routine report in 1968 by the General Accounting Office, an investigative arm of Congress, 227,000 of some 90 million gallons of waste stored this way had leaked from storage containers into the ground.

Public concern and growing government awareness of the dangers of nuclear technology led to passage of the landmark 1969 National Environmental Policy Act. Recognizing the need for people to coexist with their environment, the act ordered all government agencies to provide a written analysis of the effects on the environment of their activities and to examine alternative—and less harmful—methods of action. The following year, Congress passed the Water Quality Improvement Act, to protect the nation's water supply from various industrial hazards. The act held industry responsible for much of the damage it caused to the nation's water; in particular, it strengthened restrictions on thermal pollution from nuclear power plants.

Armed with this new legislation, environmental and public-interest groups set out afresh to stop the AEC and the nuclear industry from building more nuclear power plants. In a landmark legal battle in 1970–71, the issue of environment versus nuclear technology came to a head. The case revolved around the proposed construction by the Baltimore Gas and Electric Company of two 845 MWe units at Calvert Cliffs, Maryland, about 30 miles from Washington, D.C. Concerned about the effects of thermal pollution on Chesapeake Bay, a coalition of citizens and environmental groups called the Calvert Cliffs Coordinating Committee banded together to oppose the project. In his decision, Judge James Skelly Wright of the Court of Appeals for the

District of Columbia ruled in favor of the concerned citizens and environmentalists. Citing the National Environmental Policy Act of 1969, Judge Wright ruled that the AEC must assess the environmental impact of the proposed plant. Moreover, he ruled that the AEC would have to do the same retroactively for more than 30 reactors that had applied for licenses in the previous 2 years. As a result of this ruling, and in the face of costly delays and the prospect of prolonged court action, utilities began installing cooling towers and ponds that would cool the heated water before releasing it into rivers.

Encased in steel drums, radioactive waste material from AEC and other nuclear facilities is buried at an Idaho site. In 1968, a routine congressional investigation found that radioactive debris disposed of in this way had leaked into the ground at certain dumping sites.

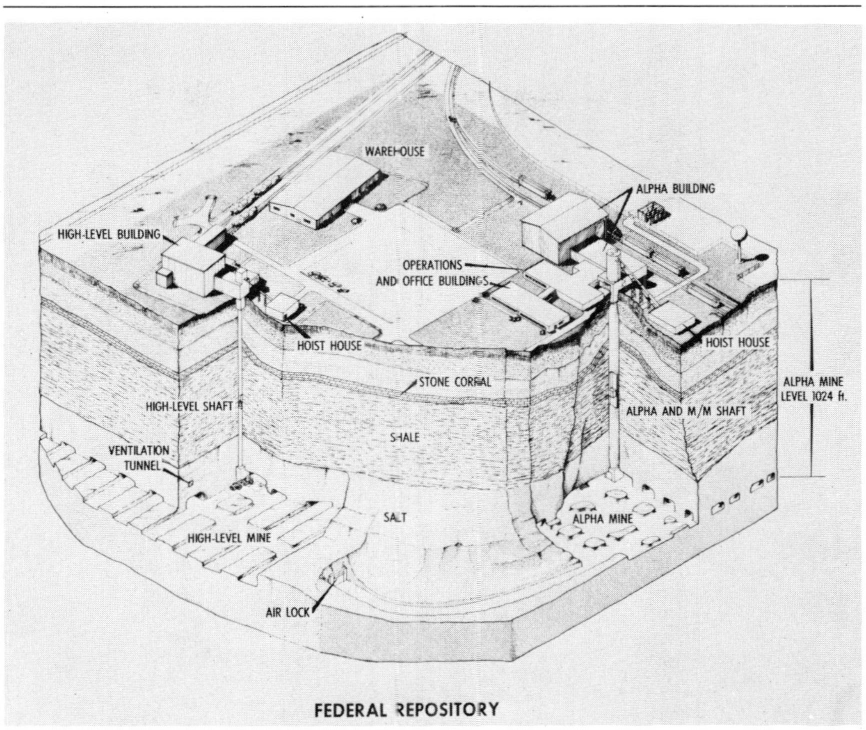

A cutaway view of the proposed radioactive-waste burial site in Lyons, Kansas. In 1970, the AEC intended to use the site—a salt mine—to dispose of nuclear waste in caverns 1,000 feet underground until the year 2000.

On the question of waste disposal, public opposition dealt the AEC and nuclear industry another blow. The General Accounting Office's report of leaking nuclear waste tanks led the AEC to announce in 1970 that it had chosen the nation's first radioactive waste disposal site: a salt mine in Lyons, Kansas. However, Kansas officials rose in resistance. William H. Hambleton, director of the Kansas Geological Survey, challenged initial studies that had determined the site's adequacy. He argued that disintegration of the storage containers, which would remain dangerously radioactive for thousands of years, could cause enough heat to crack rock formations around the salt deposits. Eventually, this could lead to geysers spewing radioactive salt.

Moreover, Kansas representative Joe Skubitz complained that no plan existed to retrieve wastes in an unforeseen emergency, and Hollis Dole, assistant secretary of the Department of the Interior, raised additional

James R. Schlesinger, chairman of the AEC from 1971 to 1973, exhibits a model of the fast breeder reactor, a nuclear reactor that theoretically can produce more atomic fuel than it consumes.

environmental questions. Kansas governor Robert Docking and others applied more political pressure, but the AEC kept pushing to develop the site until May 1972, when they finally relented. AEC chairman Seaborg had left nine months earlier, in the wake of the Calvert Cliffs decision. President Richard Nixon had appointed James R. Schlesinger chairman in an effort to restore the commission's public credibility, and the new chairman now announced that aboveground waste sites would be used.

The AEC increasingly found itself at odds with a rising tide of social and political change. Environmental achievements such as the 1969 National Environmental Policy Act and the 1970 Water Quality Improvement Act made nuclear development financially less attractive and increased the complexity of regulation. Then, on June 22, 1973, a group of antinuclear environmentalists called Friends of the Earth, together with consumer activist Ralph Nader, filed suit in federal district court in Washington, D.C., against the Atomic Energy Commission. When Senator Mike Gravel of Alaska rose to speak to his colleagues in the U.S. Senate that day, he quoted the suit, saying, "A massive cover-up of most urgent reactor safety problems has been practiced by the AEC for years." The suit charged that "the lives of millions of people are being threatened by the operation of these plants." Gravel warned that nuclear power plants may "create the potential for complete and irreversible poisoning of the planet."

Even scientists, by becoming embroiled in the safety controversy, were fanning public skepticism of nuclear power. In a May 1973 editorial in the American Chemical Society's publication *Chemical Technology*, editor B. J. Luberoff wrote, "For years I've accepted nuclear energy as a splendid example of what we technologists can do. Now, quite suddenly, it scares the hell out of me!" Through their debates, the Scientists' Institute for Public Information and the Union of Concerned Scientists showed the public that, where the risks of nuclear development were concerned, even scientific experts could not agree.

The era of rapid development was over. Everywhere, it seemed, newspapers trumpeted new flaws of "Atomic Lemons," as the *Wall Street Journal* called less-than-perfect nuclear plants in a May 1973 article. That July, the Charlottesville, Virginia, *Daily Progress* printed an editorial entitled "Needed: A Nuclear Plant Moratorium." Ticking off one doubt after another, the article noted that

> A dramatic increase in cancer-related deaths in areas downstream from the Shippingport Nuclear Power Station on the Ohio River in Beaver County, Pennsylvania, has been linked to the plant.

> In 1966, a runaway reactor at the Enrico Fermi Plant [located near Detroit, Michigan] raised serious speculation as to the advisability of evacuating Detroit. . . . According to investigations conducted by consumer advocate Ralph Nader, the possibility of a recurrence of such a mishap still exists.

> Emergency core cooling systems have been found to be unacceptably unpredictable.

> At its present "state of the art," there is no known way to permanently dispose of "hot" radioactive waste, which will produce potential lethal levels of radiation for thousands of years.

Meanwhile, the price of oil had skyrocketed almost 650 percent, from $1.80 per gallon in 1970 to $11.65 in early 1973. Then, on October 18, 1973, in retaliation for U.S. support of Israel in the Yom Kippur War, the Organization

During the 1973 OPEC oil embargo the United States's oil reserves dwindled, fuel prices soared, and automobile owners woke at dawn to line up at the gas pumps. The boycott demonstrated American vulnerability to foreign energy suppliers and the need for alternative independent energy sources.

of Petroleum Exporting Countries (OPEC) announced it would stop selling oil to the United States. As a result, the nation's oil supply effectively dried up. No longer would the United States have plenty of cheap fuel for power. On the contrary, the nation's power shortage became acute as an "energy crisis" began.

Facing an urgent need for more power and craving the independence that nuclear energy could bring, the nation looked to the AEC for help. None was forthcoming. Instead, congressmen accused huge experimental nuclear plants of being "the biggest single risk that any civilization has ever taken." In March 1973, Senator Gravel introduced a bill called "The Nuclear Power Moratorium Act of 1973," a bill designed to phase out the operation, construction, and export of civilian nuclear-fission power plants by 1980.

Time was running out for the AEC. Rapid development at the expense of public confidence in regulation had taken its toll on the agency. Although the marriage of promotion and regulation had worked well in the 1950s and 1960s, it had fared badly in the early 1970s. Besieged socially and undercut politically, the AEC was disbanded in 1974. No longer would one agency handle both regulation and development of nuclear power.

In October 1974, Congress passed the Energy Reorganization Act of 1974. Divorcing regulatory duties from developmental and promotional responsibilities, the act created two separate organizations. To the new Energy Research and Development Administration it gave developmental duties—responsibility for nurturing the nuclear industry's growth. The second organization inherited the AEC's regulatory duties. Called the Nuclear Regulatory Commission, it had five commissioners who would license nuclear power facilities, safeguard public health, and perform reactor research. Serving as a watchdog, the NRC would defend environmental and public safety against the hazards of nuclear growth.

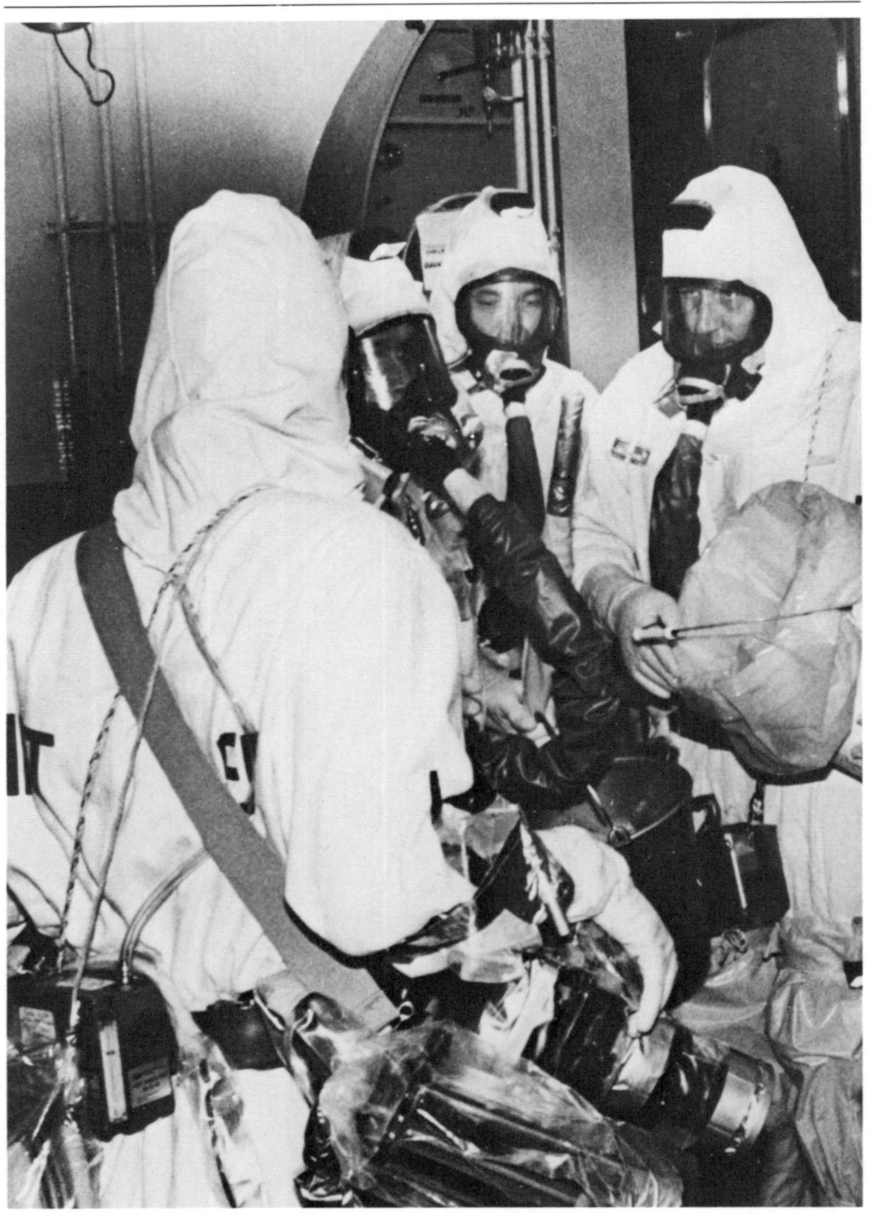

Reactor technicians prepare to enter the containment building housing the damaged Unit 2 reactor at Pennsylvania's Three Mile Island nuclear power plant. The 1979 accident at Three Mile Island was a turning point for the NRC.

THREE

Coming of Age

In January 1975, when the NRC officially came into existence, the nuclear industry was booming. Over the previous decade, it had been growing on average at least 40 percent per year, and by 1974 the large number of nuclear reactors in the planning stages brought the total number of reactors in operation, under construction, or being planned to 239. As President Gerald Ford looked ahead into the 1980s, he foresaw more of the same growth. In his 1975 State of the Union address, the president outlined a massive energy policy that called for "200 major nuclear power plants" in operation by 1985.

Although nuclear power was not the only outlet for nuclear energy, it was by far the main one. True, other uses of nuclear energy were growing, notably in medicine, which used radioactive drugs and other nuclear materials to help treat cancer and diagnose disease. Universities, too, used nuclear materials to carry on scientific research in physics, chemistry, and biology—such as the use of radioactive chemicals to track plants' absorption of a certain pesticide or to study the physiological processes of animals. However, the production of electrical power was the nuclear industry's profit-making flagship.

This meant that the NRC channeled much of its time into reactor licensing. The licensing process began once an applicant, such as a utility company, filed for a construction permit to build at a chosen site and proceeded in four steps:

• The applicant submitted an application, generally consisting of 10 or more large volumes of information relating to public and environmental health and safety. The application addressed reactor design, site considerations, hypothetical accident situations, safety features, and the area's population density, seismology (earthquake characteristics), meteorology (atmospheric and weather conditions), geology (the quality of the earth), and hydrology (underground water conditions).

• The NRC then reviewed these concerns, also examining safeguards (such as accident precautions) and business matters, specifically questions about compliance with antitrust laws, which protect trade from monopolies and unfair business practices.

• Following application and preliminary review, the Advisory Committee on Reactor Safeguards, an independent committee that counseled the NRC on the technical aspects of reactor safety, conducted a safety review.

• A three-member Atomic Safety and Licensing Board then held public hearings to provide an opportunity for the public to air complaints or concerns about the proposed project.

By the end of the licensing process, the NRC had also checked documentation of the project's financial stability. When an application received the agency's approval, construction was allowed to begin on the facility—a process that took an average of six years. About two or three years before a plant's scheduled completion, the utility applied for an operating license. Without this license, which detailed requirements for safety and environmental protection, the facility could not receive a go-ahead to operate. Again, a similar review process began anew. The NRC also held a public hearing at this point if one was requested. Then, once licensed, the utility remained under NRC surveillance.

The average "lead time"—the period from the decision to build a nuclear plant to the date it actually began producing electricity—was upwards of 10 years. Actual construction took about six years, and planning prior to that took at least two. After construction, the review process—including public hearings—and the operating-license application procedure lengthened the process by at least two more years.

If nothing else, the long lead times put great pressure on utility companies. Before a utility could decide whether a nuclear plant would be worthwhile, it had to predict electricity consumption a decade or more in advance. If the utility's forecasts were wrong, its proposed reactor might have too much—or too little—capacity. Moreover, if the NRC required design changes during construction, which it often did, the resulting delays lengthened lead time.

Construction of nuclear power plants was booming when the NRC assumed its regulatory role in 1975. The plant-construction process took approximately six years, but it could easily be lengthened by NRC-required design changes or by environmental concerns.

Often, as scientists developed safer designs and more sturdy methods of construction, the NRC required that plants under construction incorporate these new building technologies. This, of course, meant delays and costs that easily skyrocketed. The cost of building a reactor averaged some $1.2 billion per plant; a delay of three years could add another $200 million to this figure, according to some industry estimates. The average building cost rose from $313 per kWe (kilowatt of electricity) for reactors that began operating between 1971 and 1974 to $576 per kWe for reactors in the period 1977–80, according to Department of Energy statistics. And as costs rose, financial institutions became less willing to put up the needed funds.

Increasingly, electric utilities found themselves in a financial squeeze. The economic recession that followed OPEC's cutoff of oil supplies to the United States in 1973 sent the utilities into a slump. Consumers conserved electric power, demand for construction of new power plants fell off, and utilities began canceling orders for new reactors. In 1976, utilities canceled two orders for reactors, followed by six in 1977 and nine more in late 1977 and early 1978.

Other factors besides lower demand for nuclear power strongly contributed to the nuclear industry's downturn. Prime among these were safety questions nagging at the public's mind. One of the biggest dilemmas was how to control "low-level" radioactive waste, such as contaminated gloves and hand tools, contaminated vials from medicine, and filters and sludge collected after cleaning

A worker at a low-level waste dump in Idaho checks barrels for radioactive leakage. In the mid-1970s, problems at nuclear waste sites contributed to public disillusionment with the nuclear industry.

a reactor's coolant water. Throwing such trash into ordinary garbage dumps was out of the question because it was much too radioactive and potentially dangerous to public health.

Until 1970, much of the low-level waste was encased in metal barrels and sunk in more than 50 ocean dumps. But by 1980, according to the Environmental Protection Agency, about 25 percent of these barrels had leaks and were oozing radioactive material. Low-level industrial-waste dumps had been another solution, and by 1980 such sites were accepting yearly some 100,000 cubic meters of low-level waste for burial in 600-foot-long trenches 40 feet wide and 20 feet deep. But in 1975, one site in West Valley, New York, closed its doors because of water contamination problems. The same fate forced the shutdown of a dump in Morehead, Kentucky, in 1977. Two years after that, amid charges that federal regulations regarding packaging and transportation were not being followed, three other dumps—located in Beatty, Nevada; Barnwell, South Carolina; and Hanford, Washington—ordered a temporary dumping halt.

Thickener tanks at a uranium-processing plant, where uranium oxide is extracted from uranium ore to make nuclear reactor fuel. Disposal of uranium "tailings," the radioactive residue left by the extraction process, presented a serious problem to the besieged nuclear industry during the 1970s.

Uranium "tailings," bits of radioactive ore left over after uranium was processed into nuclear fuel, presented another difficult waste problem. Piles of the sandlike tailings, about 25 million tons worth milled between the early 1940s and 1970s, littered sites of old uranium mills in 8 western states. Once thought to be harmless, the tailings actually gave off low levels of radiation; people who lived near the mills were getting sick. In Mesa County in western Colorado, for example, where uranium was milled from 1951 to 1970, studies showed the acute leukemia rate to be twice the state average. Although scientists could find no proven link between the mill sites and higher cancer rates, tailings nonetheless seemed to be harmful. To prevent or minimize environmental hazards from active and inactive mill operations, Congress passed the Uranium Mill Tailings Radiation Control Act in November 1978. Besides ordering the cleanup of existing tailings, the act authorized the NRC to set stricter controls on the handling and disposal of uranium-mill waste.

With increasing public outcry over the hazards of nuclear power production, reactor safety itself became a target. Early in 1979, the Union of Concerned

The Three Mile Island nuclear power plant dominates the surrounding Pennsylvania countryside. The 1979 disaster at the plant brought nuclear development in the United States to a halt as Americans were confronted for the first time with a serious nuclear accident.

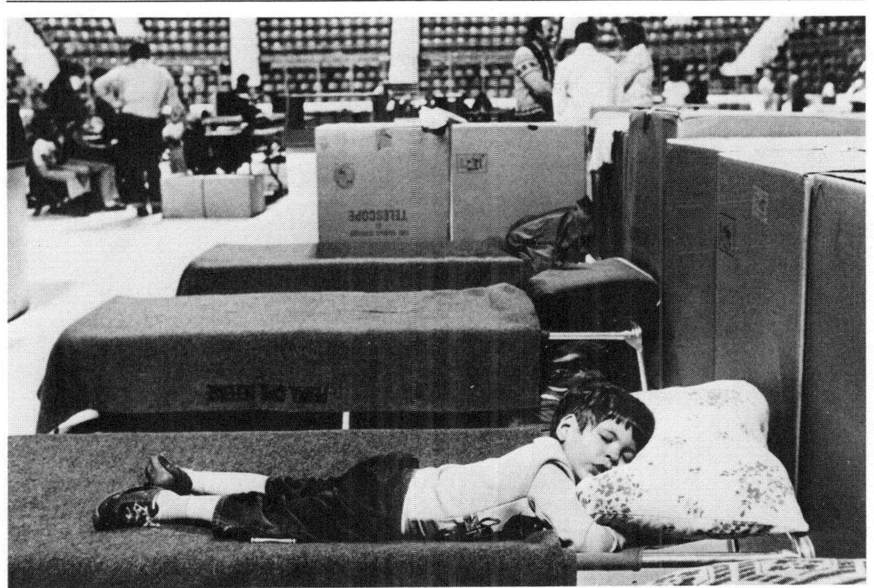

A small boy naps at an evacuation center in Hershey, Pennsylvania, after the Three Mile Island accident. Because government officials were unsure of the extent of radiation released during the event, many residents fled the area.

Scientists, a major public-policy organization critical of existing nuclear regulations, questioned safety at 16 reactors and called on the government to close them. In March, the NRC ordered five plants closed after learning that they would not be as safe during an earthquake as originally believed.

By this time, strapped financially and suffering from public skepticism, the nuclear industry's growth was slowing to a crawl. The NRC had its hands full as well. A March 1979 report by the General Accounting Office faulted the NRC for not making emergency evacuation plans part of the reactor licensing process and recommended that the 5-mile "emergency planning zone" surrounding reactors be increased to 10 miles. During the controversy over this issue, an event occurred that suddenly brought public doubt about nuclear safety and government criticism of the NRC to a head.

At 4:00 A.M. on March 28, 1979, pumps that kept cool water flowing over fuel rods in the Unit 2 reactor at the Three Mile Island nuclear plant near Harrisburg, Pennsylvania, stopped, touching off the worst nuclear reactor accident in the nation's history. With a failed cooling system, the reactor's uranium core overheated and began to melt. Radioactivity spewed into the

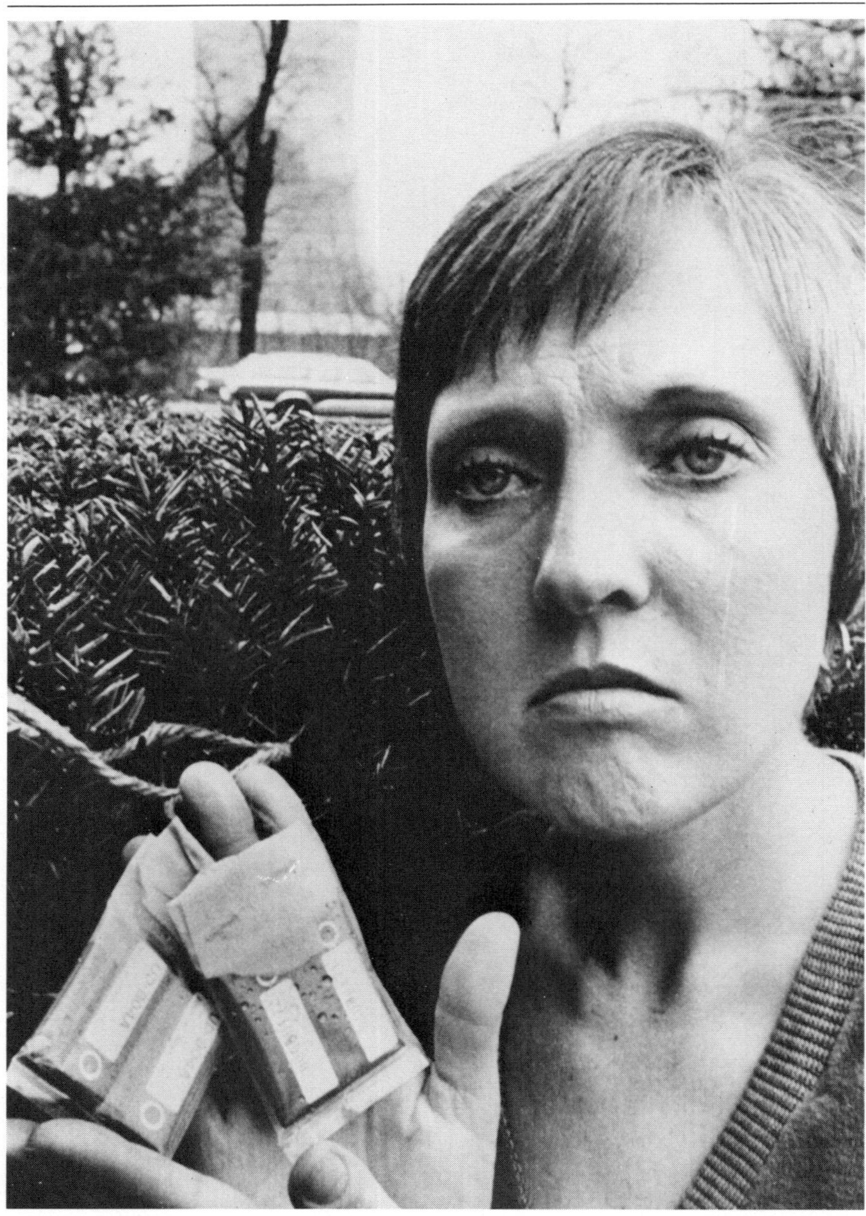

Under the shadow of a cooling tower at the Three Mile Island plant, a woman holds detectors placed in her shrubs by the NRC to monitor radiation levels. Because the TMI accident was the first nuclear disaster of its kind, its effects were difficult to predict.

atmosphere. A dangerous bubble of hydrogen gas formed within the reactor, and the threat of explosion loomed as operators tried frantically to bridle the runaway reactor. As news of the disaster spread, thousands in the area stayed home from work in fear and uncertainty, and the state's nearby capital, Harrisburg, turned into a ghost town. Many area schools canceled classes. As radioactive water and gases leaked from the facility, government officials worried about whether to evacuate residents. Within a few days, Governor Richard L. Thornburgh asked pregnant women and children within five miles of the plant to leave.

In a matter of days—after the reactor was shut down, the panic had subsided, and the more-than-$900 million mopping-up process had begun—the accident had become an indictment of the nuclear industry's operating procedures. Many viewed Three Mile Island (TMI) as a symbol of nuclear power's inherent dangers and public-health risks. Still others would use TMI to challenge the very existence of the Nuclear Regulatory Commission.

John G. Kemeny, chairman of President Jimmy Carter's Commission on the Accident at Three Mile Island, holds a copy of the commission's report. Subtitled "The Need For Change: The Legacy of TMI," the report was critical of the NRC.

In many ways, the Three Mile Island accident was a turning point, both for the NRC and for the nuclear power industry itself. After the accident, the NRC abruptly stopped issuing licenses, a halt that continued until August 1980. In the aftermath of TMI, which received international attention as the worst nuclear disaster in U.S. history, President Jimmy Carter established the Kemeny Commission, chaired by Dartmouth College president John G. Kemeny, to investigate the accident. The commission's findings were severely critical of the NRC. Among the recommendations in its 32-page report, issued on October 30, 1979, were upgrading plant safety and emergency-response plans, expanding research on the effects of radiation, tightening supervision of the training and reviewing of reactor staff, and extensively strengthening the NRC's Office of Inspection and Enforcement. The Kemeny report also strongly urged that government regulation of nuclear power concentrate on safety rather than on licensing. Most drastic, however, was the commission's recommendation that the five-member independent NRC be abolished and replaced by an executive-branch agency headed by a single administrator, who would be appointed by the president. Quoting from the report, Kemeny himself

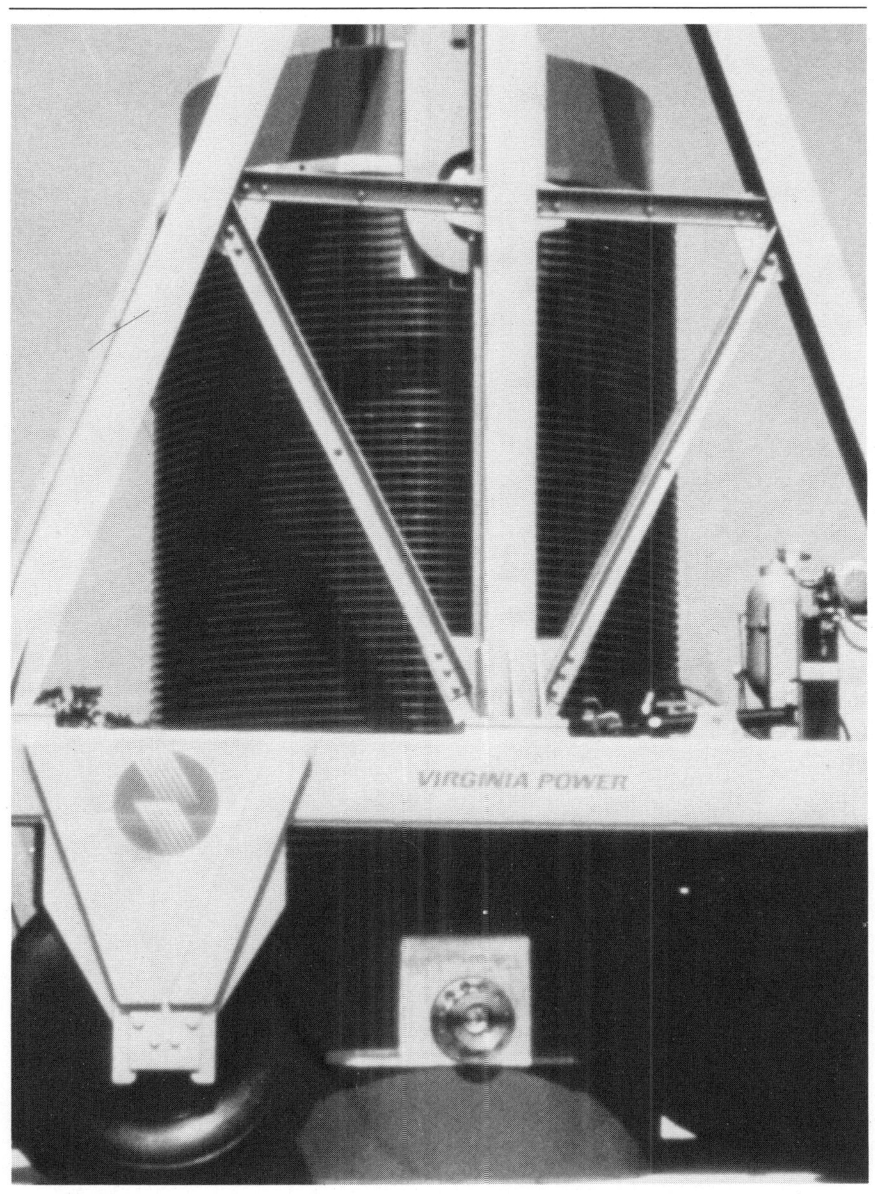

An aboveground cask was approved by the NRC for the storage of high-level radioactive waste at the Surry power station near Richmond, Virginia. The casks, each 16 feet high and 8 feet in diameter with 15-inch-thick iron walls, are mounted on a pad made of reinforced concrete.

told the House Subcommittee on Energy Research and Production, "We are convinced that unless portions of the industry and its regulatory agency undergo fundamental changes, they will, over time, totally destroy public confidence, and hence, they will be responsible for the elimination of nuclear power as a viable source of energy."

In March 1980 President Carter sent a plan to Congress incorporating this advice. Although he agreed with the general thrust of the Kemeny Commission's findings, the president rejected the commission's call to replace the NRC; instead, he proposed to strengthen the agency by restructuring its existing management. This restructuring increased the chairman's authority, allowing him alone to control staff operations and to direct the commission's response to a nuclear emergency. Before TMI, the commission as a group had shared such supervision.

In the wake of TMI, Congress passed renewed legislation to protect the environment from nuclear hazards. In 1980, Congress enacted the Low-level Radioactive Waste Policy Act, which allowed each state to provide for low-level waste disposal at regional disposal facilities. Then, in 1982, noting that "the most pressing public issue regarding nuclear power [prior to TMI] was the safe disposal of radioactive waste," Congress passed the Nuclear Waste Policy Act, geared toward the safe disposal of high-level radioactive waste, extremely dangerous waste produced within reactors and from the reprocessing of highly radioactive used (also called spent or irradiated) nuclear fuel. This law established a federal program for interim storage of spent fuel and accelerated research and development of radioactive-waste disposal technologies. Spent nuclear fuel contains useful plutonium and uranium that can be reused if the spent fuel is reprocessed; however, an industry capable of doing the reprocessing did not exist in 1982, and most of the spent fuel from commercial operations at that time was stored, awaiting the coming of a reprocessing industry.

Meanwhile, reactor safety questions persisted in the public's mind. On April 26, 1986, these doubts turned into alarm. On the Pripyat River, about 80 miles north of Kiev, the third largest city in the Soviet Union, the world's worst nuclear reactor accident to date occurred. At 1:24 A.M. there were two explosions in the core of the fourth unit of the Chernobyl nuclear power plant, located in a thinly populated Ukrainian farming region. At first, scientists in Sweden, Finland, and Denmark, detecting abnormally high radioactivity levels, suspected that material was leaking from one of their own reactors. But in fact it was spewing from the Chernobyl plant, damaged and fiercely ablaze with 100-foot-high flames. After the accident, the *New York Times* quoted Soviet

The damaged reactor (center) at the Chernobyl nuclear power plant in the Soviet Union. The explosion and fire at Chernobyl in 1986 completely destroyed the reactor, caused deaths and widespread illness, and raised radiation levels throughout Europe.

Communist party leader Boris N. Yeltsin as saying that approximately 49,000 people were evacuated from the area, 197 people were hospitalized, and 20 to 25 were critically ill. In fact, a total of 31 people died as a result of the accident. In addition, water reservoirs near the crippled plant were contaminated.

As the Chernobyl reactor burned, winds first carried radioactive substances northwest toward Scandinavia, then blew them southwest toward Romania and Yugoslavia. Polish television warned citizens to avoid drinking milk from grazing cows, which could be contaminated by particles of radioactive iodine that had been detected in Warsaw. Scientists in Stockholm, Sweden, said the accident showered Scandinavia with traces of 14 radioactive substances, some likely to persist for a long time. The Italian government banned the sale of leafy vegetables for two weeks and advised against giving children fresh milk. West Germany impounded fresh milk from several regions suspected of contamination. In the United States, the government advised women of childbearing age

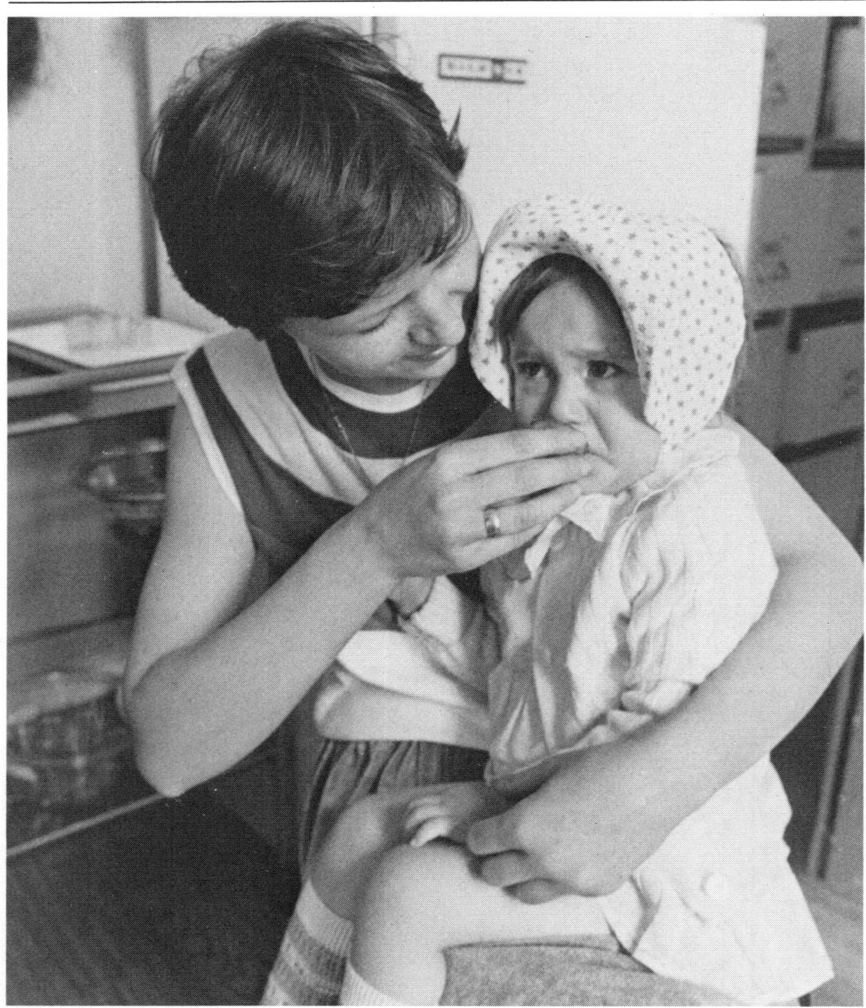

A young Polish girl cries as she is fed an iodine solution to counteract the effects of the radiation that swept across Poland in the aftermath of the Chernobyl accident. Chernobyl's worldwide repercussions gave the NRC an opportunity to examine the effects of a nuclear disaster and to evaluate its own safety systems.

not to travel to Poland because of potential radiation hazards from the Chernobyl fallout. As a safety precaution, the governments of Canada, Australia, and Britain evacuated children from diplomatic posts.

Worldwide, the Chernobyl accident had a sobering impact. After the disaster, NRC staff collected and analyzed data, seeking to better understand the causes and consequences of the disaster. From August 25 to 29, 1986, the NRC participated in a conference convened by Soviet authorities and the International Atomic Energy Agency in Vienna, Austria, at which Soviet experts presented a detailed report on the progression of the accident and its repercussions in the Soviet Union. Then the NRC conducted reviews of the accident, the design of the Chernobyl reactor, its bypassed safety systems (Chernobyl operators had apparently shut off emergency equipment during a test and then ignored subsequent warning signals, leading authorities to blame the accident on human error), emergency planning, and other aspects of the disaster to better inform reactor operation and safety precautions in the United States.

Although the Chernobyl reactor and U.S. reactors had basic design differences (for example, Soviet reactors have no containment dome, which in United States reactors helps to prevent the escape of radioactive gases after an accident), NRC evaluation of the Soviet incident helped to put the U.S. nuclear program and its regulatory systems into perspective. Three Mile Island and other less-dramatic nuclear accidents had increased American awareness of the dangers of nuclear power, but the Chernobyl accident—with its wide media coverage and severe worldwide repercussions—gave U.S. officials their first real opportunity to study the effects of a nuclear disaster on human and environmental health and to evaluate their own safety systems and evacuation plans.

All this had an effect on the NRC as well as on the nation's nuclear industry. In 1986, facing a maturing—rather than growing—nuclear industry at home, and facing skepticism about nuclear power nationally as well as abroad, the NRC made plans to reorganize its regulatory structure. Because few new reactors were in demand, the bulk of NRC work shifted from licensing new reactors to monitoring and regulating existing ones—a change in priority that had been suggested by the Kemeny Commission in 1979. Accordingly, the NRC updated and upgraded, responding to the needs of the nation and keeping pace with needs of the nuclear industry. How it is able to accomplish this is in large part owing to the way in which it is organized.

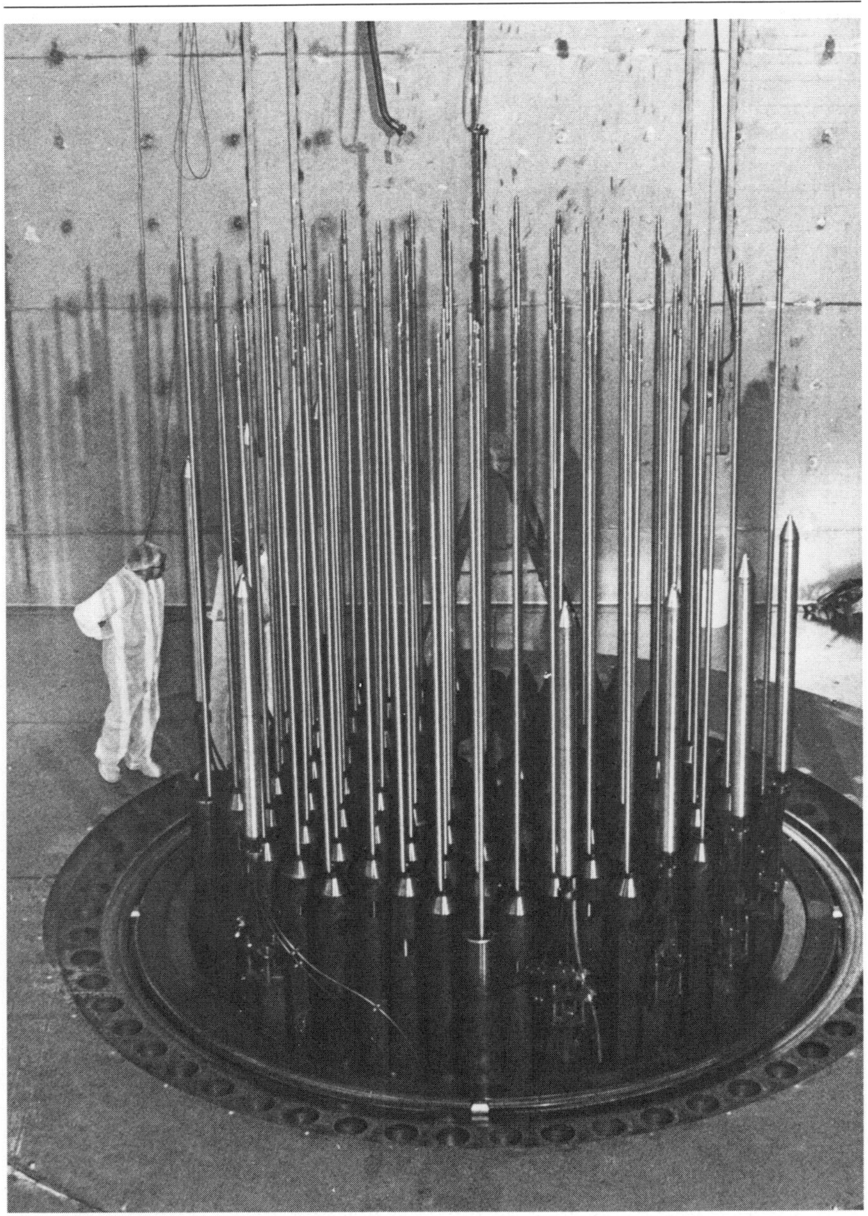

Control rods protruding from the top of a reactor vessel dwarf a pair of nuclear power plant workers. Because of the potentially dangerous nature of nuclear power production, the NRC keeps a close watch over reactor operation and employee conduct.

FOUR

Regulating Nuclear Power

The Nuclear Regulatory Commission has five members, each nominated by the president for a five-year term and subject to Senate confirmation. From these commissioners, the president appoints a chairman. Each year, one commissioner's term comes to an end and he is replaced by a new member.

The NRC's five commissioners administer the agency, with ultimate authority and responsibility for regulatory decisions from the construction of nuclear power plants and the acceptable risk of a plant to fish ecology to cleanup after an accident. For expertise in specific areas, however, the commissioners rely on three offices to make crucial regulatory decisions: the Advisory Committee on Reactor Safeguards, the Atomic Safety and Licensing Board Panel, and the Atomic Safety and Licensing Appeal Panel. Much like a panel of judges in a court, these three offices hear cases and render rulings.

The Advisory Committee on Reactor Safeguards consists of 15 scientists and engineers who advise the commission on safety aspects of proposed and existing nuclear facilities. The committee also advises on the adequacy of proposed reactor-safety standards. Each year, the committee submits to Congress its continuing study of reactor safety.

The Atomic Safety and Licensing Board Panel (ASLBP) is made up of lawyers and others with technical expertise in various fields. As of September

At their 1975 swearing-in ceremony, the NRC's first five commissioners pledged to lead the new agency in licensing and regulating nuclear facilities and to take steps to safeguard public health and environmental safety.

1986, the panel included 21 permanent and 25 part-time administrative judges, including 16 lawyers, 15 environmental scientists, 7 engineers, 5 physicists, a physician, an economist, and a chemist. When a utility or other applicant requests a license, the commissioners select a three-member panel from this group to conduct public hearings. Each panel is chosen according to the individual judges' professional experience and expertise. In general, a licensing board consists of a lawyer, who acts as chairman, a nuclear engineer or reactor physicist, and an environmental scientist. A hearing on an application may require several phases, each focusing on one licensing concern at a time. For instance, separate issues may include health, safety, security, environmental impact, and emergency planning. The panel may also make intermediate or final decisions on the license, as the commission authorizes. In 1986, the ASLBP conducted 58 proceedings involving nuclear power facilities and authorized 6 nuclear power plant units for final licensing.

The Atomic Safety and Licensing Appeal Panel, a three-member appeals board, reviews licensing board decisions that are in dispute. If either side wishes to further contest the appeal board's ruling, it must appeal directly to the commissioners.

Commission Staff

Also a step down from the commissioners and aiding them in a similar fashion are the commission staff, or offices that perform administrative functions: the Office of the General Counsel (the commission's legal adviser); the Office of Governmental and Public Affairs (a liaison with Congress and the public); the Office of Inspector and Auditor (an internal quality-control arm); and the Office of the Secretary (general manager). These staff offices inform and advise the commissioners regarding public activities and legal matters.

The Office of the General Counsel is the NRC's chief legal adviser. As such, the general counsel helps in reviewing appeal board decisions and rule-making proceedings and drafts legal documents needed to carry out the commission's decisions. The general counsel acts as representative for the commission in court proceedings, often in concert with the Department of Justice. The general counsel also provides legal analysis of proposed legislation and assists in drafting legislation.

The NRC's recent reorganization, which took effect in 1987, created the Office of Governmental and Public Affairs. This office incorporates the former offices of Congressional Affairs, Public Affairs, State Programs, and International Programs and reports directly to the chairman. In daily contacts with news media, at NRC meetings and at hearings, the office keeps up a steady stream of information to the public. Through press releases to news organizations, the scientific community, universities, and the general public, the office spreads news of commission programs, rulings, public hearings, proposed fines against licensees, and other agency activities. This office is also the commission's chief adviser on congressional matters, coordinating the agency's congressional-relations activities and maintaining liaison for the commission with congressional committees and individual congressmen. The three principal congressional oversight groups with which the NRC works are the Senate Subcommittee on Nuclear Regulation (a division of the Committee on Environment and Public Works); the House Subcommittee on Energy and the Environment (under the Committee on Interior and Insular Affairs); and the House Subcommittee on Energy and Power (under the Committee on Energy and Commerce). The NRC also works alongside congressional committees concerned with international relations, energy research and development, government affairs, and other concerns.

New York governor Mario Cuomo testifies at an NRC public-affairs hearing in 1987. The agency conducts such hearings to address concerns about nuclear development and to keep the public abreast of NRC and licensee activities.

The Office of Governmental and Public Affairs also performs the duties of the former Office of International Programs, supervising programs of international nuclear safety cooperation and maintaining links with foreign regulatory agencies. During 1986, for example, it supervised NRC tracking of recorded radiation levels in various countries after the nuclear disaster at the Chernobyl plant. The NRC provided regulatory authorities in other nations with this information to help them evaluate and project the accident's effects on public health. The office also coordinated NRC participation in the post-Chernobyl international conference in Vienna, Austria, in August 1986.

In addition, the Office of Governmental and Public Affairs carries out duties previously performed by the Office of State Programs, which directed regulatory relationships with state governments and organizations and with interstate bodies. Since Three Mile Island and the upsurge of public interest in nuclear-safety issues, many state governments have chosen not to depend on the NRC alone for information on the nuclear facilities within their borders. Under the State Agreements Program, a formal agreement between the NRC and 28 states under which the states have assumed certain regulatory responsibilities at nuclear facilities, state officials can routinely stay apprised of the status of specific facilities in their states. The NRC also provides technical assistance to Agreement States, such as aid to Mississippi in its review of an application for use of radioisotopes in offshore waters; to North Carolina in its review of an application for a nuclear pharmacy license; and to Kentucky in its review of an application for uses of radioisotopes in laboratory animals.

The Office of Inspector and Auditor (OIA) looks into allegations of NRC employee misconduct. Its responsibility is to assure the integrity of all NRC operations, referring criminal matters to the Department of Justice and working with law-enforcement agencies. In addition, the OIA conducts the NRC's internal audit activities and hears any concerns employees might have about commission activities. During 1986, the office issued 21 audit reports containing 79 recommendations aimed at improving various NRC operations and employee conduct. It also issued 52 investigative reports in answer to allegations of misconduct and referred 22 reports to the Department of Justice for review and possible criminal prosecution. For example, a March 1986 report criticized the NRC's handling of allegations of misconduct at California's Diablo Canyon nuclear power station. In this incident, the identity of an employee who complained of misconduct at the plant and desired to remain anonymous was revealed. After its investigation of this breach of confidentiality and other flaws in the reviewing of complaints at the NRC's San Francisco regional office, the OIA made 15 recommendations to improve the handling of such situations.

Nuclear Power: How a Reactor Works

Since 1951, when it was first used to generate electricity, nuclear energy has grown to become a mainstay of power production in the United States. Reactor technology has become increasingly sophisticated—scientists are developing different types of reactors and fuels and are researching methods of atomic reaction that will produce heat energy. Nuclear heat is used just like heat is in a conventionally fueled power facility—to generate electricity.

Approximately 15 percent of all electricity consumed by American homes and businesses is now produced by nuclear power plants. The most common type of nuclear reactor used to generate commercial electricity in the United States is the *pressurized water reactor* (see diagram). A nuclear reaction takes place within the *reactor core*, which is loaded with *fuel rods*—12-foot-long, half-inch-diameter zirconium alloy tubes containing uranium dioxide pellets. Two hundred of these rods form an *array*, or one *subassembly*; a typical fuel core contains 150 to 200 subassemblies. The core is encased in a steel tank called a *pressure vessel*.

To understand how a nuclear reactor works, one needs a grasp of the basic principles of atomic structure. At the center of each atom of uranium is a nucleus, a core of positively charged protons and neutral (uncharged) neutrons. When the atomic nucleus is bombarded by additional neutrons, it splits into smaller fragments. This process, called *fission*, releases heat energy and additional neutrons, which in turn strike other atomic nuclei and cause them to undergo fission in a *chain reaction*.

Pressurized Water Reactor

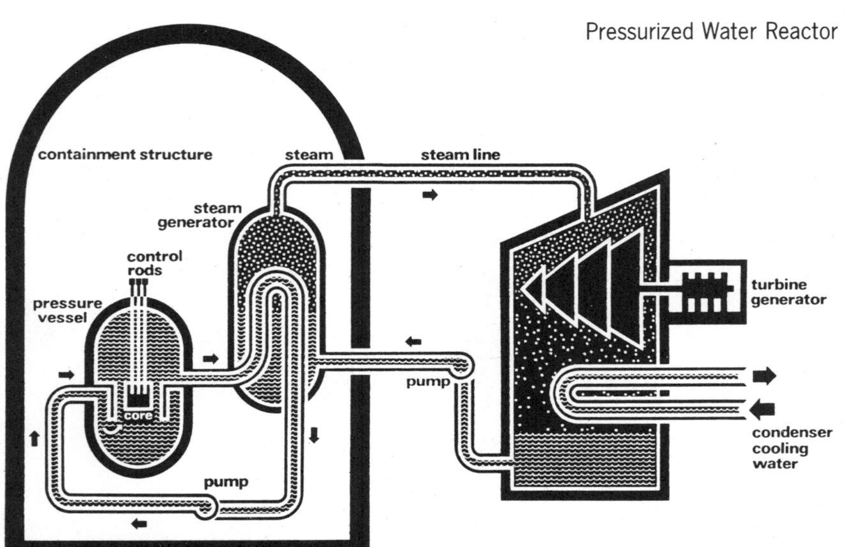

An atomic bomb explosion is caused by nuclear fission in an uncontrolled chain reaction; however, in the controlled setting of a nuclear reactor, fission can be regulated to produce a steady flow of heat energy. This is accomplished by inserting *control rods* into the reactor core. The control rods are made of a material (usually cadmium or boron, encased in zirconium alloy tubes) that absorbs neutrons and, by rendering them unable to strike and split additional nuclei, slows the rate of fission. Control rods can be inserted into the reactor vessel as needed to sustain constant fission.

Water surrounding the fuel core serves as both a *moderator,* slowing down the neutrons so that they may be captured by atomic nuclei, and a *coolant,* absorbing the heat produced by fission. In a *pressurized water reactor,* water circulating through the hot core is kept under pressure, which prevents it from boiling. This superheated water is pumped into pipes through a steam generator, where it heats separately circulating nonpressurized water into steam. The steam propels a turbine that drives an electric generator; it then passes through a condenser, where it is cooled and recirculated through the system as water. In a *boiling water reactor,* the other type of power-generating reactor in operation in the United States, the water circulating through the reactor core is allowed to boil. The resulting steam drives the turbines and is then condensed and circulated through the hot core once again.

As long as the rate of fission is kept constant and the fuel core is kept cool, the reactor provides a trouble-free source of heat energy. Sensitive instruments monitor conditions within the reactor and call attention to any unexpected change in water flow, power level, reactor pressure, or the temperature of the coolant leaving the core. If any of these conditions deviate from their normal range of operation, reactor personnel are alerted and will manually shut down the reactor by inserting control rods. The monitoring system is also able to activate an automatic reactor shutdown.

Once a reactor's power is shut off, steps must be taken to control the still-present heat of radioactive decay. An overheated reactor can melt the fuel core and lead to the release of dangerous radioactivity into the atmosphere. To prevent such a disaster, the reactor's cooling system continues to pump water over the fuel core even after the reactor is shut down. In the unlikely event of cooling-system malfunction, the *emergency core-cooling system*, a sophisticated auxiliary heat-removal system, automatically fills the reactor vessel with water from flood tanks. If by this time the fuel core has already begun to melt, the thick-walled reactor vessel will contain any radioactive leakage. In addition, the containment structure—a steel-reinforced concrete dome that houses the entire system and withstands high internal pressure—prevents radioactive gases from being released into the atmosphere.

The Browns Ferry nuclear power plant in Athens, Alabama, was the first nuclear plant constructed by the Tennessee Valley Authority. The NRC's Office of Special Projects handles licensing and inspection efforts at TVA facilities.

Operations

NRC operations themselves—the "nuts and bolts" of the NRC's regulatory functions—are performed further down the organizational pyramid under the direction of the executive director for operations. As the commission's chief administrator and operations officer, the executive director for operations reports directly to the commission chairman and is assisted by a number of staff offices: the Office of Consolidation and the Office of Special Projects (both created in 1987); the Office of Administration and Resources Management; the Office of Small and Disadvantaged Business Utilization and Civil Rights; the Office for Analysis and Evaluation of Operational Data; the Office of Investigations; the Office of Personnel; and five Regional Offices.

The Three Mile Island accident in 1979 showed the need for more efficient communication within the NRC; accordingly, the agency initiated steps to consolidate its staff into one headquarters, located in Rockville, Maryland. The Office of Consolidation is responsible for supervising the completion of this plan. Currently, 1,400 employees work in one building in Rockville; a second building is under construction to house the Operations Center staff, now located in Bethesda, Maryland. The NRC projects a total of 2,400 employees at its completed Rockville headquarters.

The Office of Special Projects manages the NRC's licensing and inspection efforts for the Tennessee Valley Authority and Comanche Peak (Glen Rose, Texas) nuclear facilities. The Office of Administration and Resources Management handles the agency's administrative work, including financial duties such as accounting and budget, computer and telecommunications systems super-

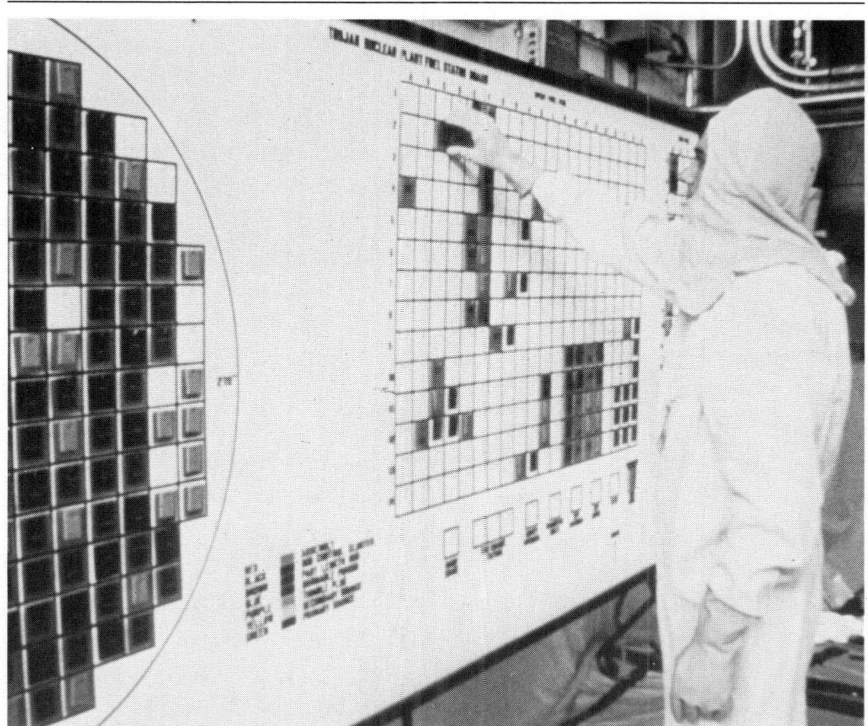

Reactor staff carefully monitor the progress of a refueling operation on a status board. Reactor personnel undergo a lengthy training process and are subject to periodic relicensing examinations by the NRC regional offices.

vision, and payroll. The Office of Small and Disadvantaged Business Utilization and Civil Rights assures the fair treatment of small businesses with whom the NRC deals and develops NRC policy concerning equal employment opportunity and affirmative-action programs.

The Office for Analysis and Evaluation of Operational Data collects, stores, and retrieves data associated with licensed activities. Using vast, computerized storage-and-retrieval systems, the office analyzes and evaluates the operational experience of nuclear plants and feeds the results back to NRC staff involved in licensing, standards, and inspections. By gathering and encoding enormous amounts of technical information from the nation's nuclear plants, the office can track and analyze events such as "scrams" (emergency reactor shutdowns), losses of safety functions, and threats to plant safety. The 1979 establishment of this office was one of the commission's earliest major steps toward improving the ways one plant's operating experience could be used to identify and resolve potential safety problems in other plants.

The Office of Investigations is an external quality-control arm. If a licensee, applicant, equipment supplier, or a contractor hired by any of these outside businesses is alleged to have done something wrong, this office conducts an investigation. (Any alleged wrongdoing by NRC staff themselves or by an NRC-hired contractor is investigated by the Office of Inspector and Auditor.) The Office of Investigations steps in when asked by the NRC commissioners, the executive director for operations, the regional administrators, or on its own initiative and reports its findings directly to the commission. At any one time, the office's caseload is about 175 cases. Approximately 35 professional investigators, including some recruited from federal law-enforcement agencies, make up its staff.

In fiscal year 1986, the Office of Investigations opened 95 new cases, bringing the total number of cases opened since the office's inception in 1982 to 854. Of the 141 cases closed that year, the NRC referred 11 to the Department of Justice for possible prosecution, and by year's end 5 more were pending before grand juries.

For example, the Office of Investigations looked into allegations that Topping Associates/American Filter Company had supplied commercial-grade filters to the Calvert Cliffs, Maryland, nuclear power plant instead of the nuclear-grade filters that are produced specifically for the needs of nuclear industry. In December 1985, the president of Topping was sentenced to one year's probation, $34,000 in damages, and a $1,000 fine after conviction on a related count of mail fraud. After another of the office's investigations, FBI

An operator in the control room of a nuclear power plant.

agents arrested a materials licensee on March 26, 1986, and charged him with illegal possession of the radioactive material americium-241 and with making false statements to the NRC concerning his possession of the material.

The Office of Personnel provides support to the main NRC offices in staffing, recruitment, organization, training and evaluation, and other staff-related functions. This office also handles labor-relations issues for the NRC.

The Comanche Peak steam electric station in Texas was the subject of a 1985 investigation by the Office of Nuclear Reactor Regulation. Responding to charges of poor-quality construction in the plant's Unit 1 reactor, the office sent a team of consultants to the site to verify the safety of the plant's design.

The NRC also maintains regional offices, five arms of the executive director reaching throughout the nation. These offices—located in Philadelphia, Pennsylvania; Atlanta, Georgia; Chicago, Illinois; Dallas, Texas; and San Francisco, California—carry out on a local level the NRC's regulatory duties, at times hand in hand with the nation's nuclear power plants in operation or under construction.

The regional offices also conduct examinations and issue licenses for nuclear reactor operators. The actual training of these workers takes place at schools run by the nuclear industry itself. (For example, General Electric and Westinghouse each have their own training program.) A prospective nuclear reactor operator must have a high-school diploma and demonstrate a general aptitude for technical and mechanical skills. An applicant must also be sponsored by a particular utility; after licensing, the operator will only be eligible to work at the reactor for which he or she has trained.

The three- to four-year training period for reactor operators includes academic coursework in subjects such as physics and practice on a reactor simulator (much like the training an airline pilot receives on a flight simulator). At the end of the training period, the sponsoring utility sends a certified letter to the appropriate NRC regional office stating that the student has had the proper training and is ready to be tested. The applicant then undergoes an extensive examination consisting of written and oral questions and a practical test on a simulator. Before licensing, the applicant must also undergo a complete physical and psychological examination and pass a drug test. Once licensed, the operator is required to submit to periodic inspections and relicensing by the NRC regional office.

Program Offices

Three offices under the executive director for operations perform much of the NRC's technical regulatory work. Known as "program offices," the Office of Nuclear Reactor Regulation, the Office of Nuclear Material Safety and Safeguards, and the Office of Nuclear Regulatory Research were all created by the Energy Reorganization Act of 1974.

The Office of Nuclear Reactor Regulation (NRR) reviews applications for construction permits and licenses nuclear power reactors as well as reactors used in testing and research. Currently, there are approximately 110 power reactors licensed to operate in the United States and approximately 30 licensed nonpower reactors, which are used in nuclear research, training, and testing.

At the end of 1986, the NRR was reviewing license applications for 24 nuclear units under construction; the following year, the office granted 8 operating licenses. In 1987, the Office of Nuclear Reactor Regulation was reorganized to reflect the shift in the agency's work load away from conducting licensing reviews toward ensuring the safety of reactors already in operation. (In 1986, for instance, although the office reviewed applications for operating licenses or construction permits submitted in previous years, it actually received no new applications.)

While reviewing license applications, the office must often resolve any questions that arise before it can make a decision. For example, as construction of the Comanche Peak steam electric station Unit 1 in Glen Rose, Texas, neared completion in 1985, questions were raised about the quality of construction. The NRR dispatched a technical review team consisting of more than 50 consultants and technical experts from the NRR, its regional offices, and national laboratories to the site to investigate these allegations. After four months, the team documented their findings in five Supplemental Safety Evaluation Reports. Meanwhile, the Atomic Safety and Licensing Board and a specially appointed Comanche Peak Independent Assessment Program reviewed additional concerns about the plant's design and construction. In response to the concerns raised by these investigations, the applicant, Texas Utilities, submitted plans that demonstrated the adequacy of the plant's design and construction. The NRC reviewed those plans and gave its approval. By year's end, under the NRC's eye, detailed reverification of design and reinspection of construction was under way.

In 1986, the NRC ordered the owner of the Diablo Canyon Unit 1 nuclear power plant in Diablo Canyon, California, to reevaluate the plant's seismic (earthquake-related) design basis in consideration of new data. In response to the order, the utility's license holder, Pacific Gas & Electric Company, organized a field trip in conjunction with NRC consultants including experts from the U.S. Geological Survey and the University of Nevada at Reno. The team instituted an ongoing field study to investigate the geologic character of the region around Diablo Canyon—in particular, the area's fault lines (geologic "fractures" in rock that are susceptible to earthquakes).

To assure environmental protection, the NRR prepares environmental-impact reviews in connection with operating-license applications. In 1985, the office completed five such reviews, addressing environmental issues from noise pollution (annoying and distracting noise) to ecology. In two of the reviews—of the Beaver Valley Unit 2 in Shippingport, Pennsylvania, and the Alvin W. Vogtle, Jr., plant units 1 and 2 in Waynesboro, Georgia—the NRC

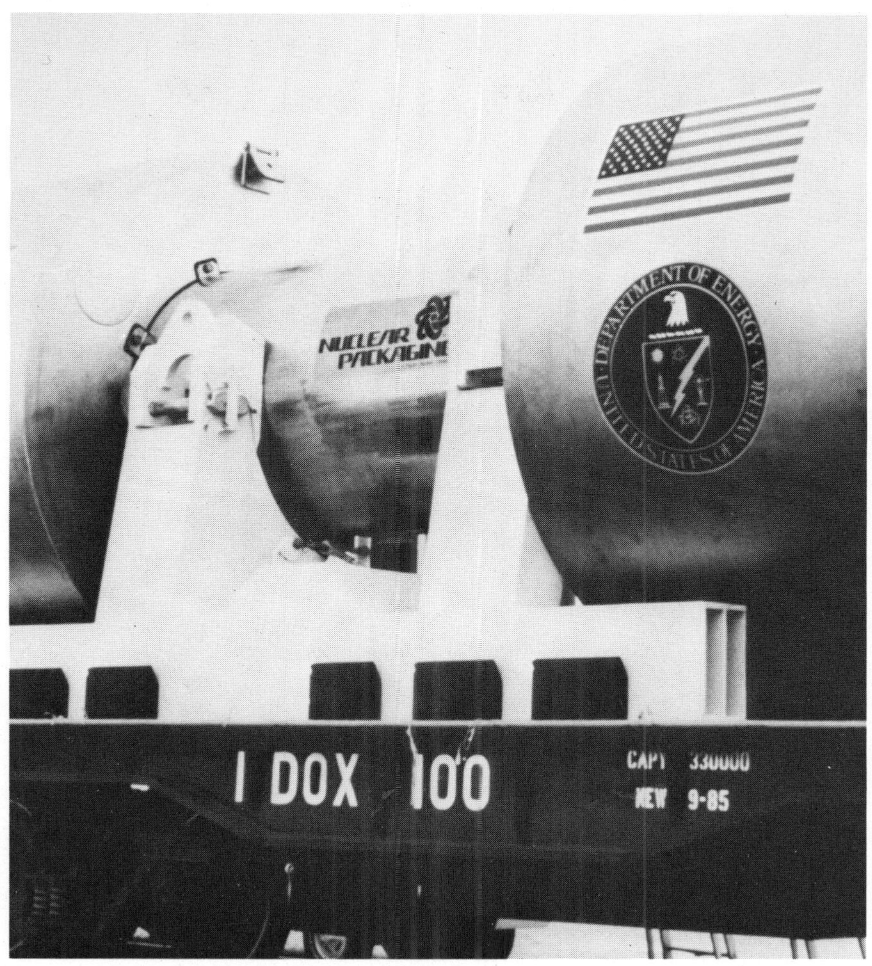

One of the specially designed railroad containers used to remove fuel from the damaged Three Mile Island reactor. The Office of Nuclear Material Safety and Safeguards conducted extensive tests on the steel cask before giving it final approval in 1986.

found that plant noise levels could be bothersome to nearby neighborhoods. The Final Environmental Statement recommended that operations be monitored and corrective action considered if the noise proved excessive.

The office also identified a potential problem with the water-cooling system at the Vogtle plant. Large clam populations in the nearby Savannah River had infested other water-intake systems in the area, and the NRR was afraid a

71

similar problem might occur in the Vogtle plant's water system. One solution to the problem was to chlorinate the cooling water, which would kill the clams; however, this could endanger other living organisms when the chlorinated water was later discharged downstream. After careful study, NRC scientists predicted in a Final Environmental Statement that the impact of these discharges would be insignificant.

The NRR also handles projects such as the ongoing cleanup at Three Mile Island and monitors crucial reactor maintenance. According to the NRC's Maintenance and Surveillance Program Plan, which evaluates the effectiveness of maintenance in the nuclear power industry, a high percentage of plant-operations failure results from improper upkeep of facilities.

The NRC's 1987 reorganization incorporated the duties of the former Office of Inspection and Enforcement—responsible for policing the nuclear industry— into the NRR. The NRR is now charged with protecting public health and safety by ensuring compliance of licensees with NRC requirements. When rules are not followed, the office first issues a "notice of violation." Repeat offenders receive civil penalties, such as fines, and in extreme cases the NRC may suspend or revoke licenses or shut down a licensee's operations altogether. In 1986 alone, the Office of Inspection and Enforcement had imposed 96 civil penalties and collected more than $3 million in fines. For example, the Commonwealth Edison Company was fined $37,500 for failing to maintain adequate control over a security-badge system at its Seneca, Illinois, facility. The NRC also fined Princeton University $2,000 for violations after an individual received a skin exposure of 38 "rems" (a rem is a measure of biological damage from radiation exposure) in a laboratory. Also in 1986, the NRC issued 10 "enforcement orders," which are stronger than violation notices, to encourage compliance with regulations; in 1985, one such order suspended the license of a medical research facility in Vermont for violations including the unauthorized use of radioactive material.

The Office of Nuclear Material Safety and Safeguards (NMSS) is similar in nature to the NRR, but it regulates nuclear materials and facilities other than reactors. The NMSS is responsible for licensing and regulating facilities and materials used to process, transport, and handle nuclear materials, as well as for the disposal of nuclear waste. It oversees the storage of spent reactor fuel and the production and use of "by-product material," radioisotopes produced by reactors.

The NMSS is consulted when nuclear fuel or waste must be transported from a reactor to a laboratory or storage facility—as with damaged nuclear fuel created by the Three Mile Island disaster. On April 11, 1986, the NMSS approved a railroad container for use to transport damaged fuel from the core of Three Mile Island Unit 2 to the U.S. Department of Energy's Idaho National Engineering Laboratory near Pocatello, Idaho. There, scientists would analyze the fuel to gain a better understanding of the TMI accident and to aid future cleanup procedures. The fuel container, known as a 125-B cask, had shields of lead and stainless steel and looked something like a 17-foot, 91-ton barbell. Before approving the cask for use, the office conducted tests on a quarter-scale model, a copy identical in every way except size. Tests included dropping the model from 30 feet, important in determining the container's safety and strength.

Nuclear material is also transported on the nation's highways, often accompanied by security vehicles for added protection against possible theft or sabotage. In 1985, the NMSS approved 46 transportation routes within the United States for this purpose. But regardless of the method of transportation, the NMSS does not work alone. In most cases, as with the damaged-fuel transport from Three Mile Island, the office works alongside the U.S. Department of Transportation and with state transportation and nuclear regulatory agencies.

The NMSS is also responsible for regulating uranium-recovery facilities, which include mining operations and mills. The NRC Uranium Recovery Field Office is located in Denver, Colorado, near the heart of the uranium industry (located mainly in New Mexico, Colorado, Wyoming, and Utah). Between 1984 and 1985, the NMSS conducted or assisted in 26 inspections of uranium-recovery facilities, of which there were 32 licensed nationwide by 1986.

Because nuclear material can be valuable to nations not yet in possession of nuclear technology, to terrorists, and to others, the NMSS reviews and assesses safeguards against potential threats, theft, and sabotage of licensed facilities, including reactors. The office conducts practice safety exercises, which sometimes involve firing weapons. Law-enforcement agencies such as the FBI may join these exercises.

The Office of Nuclear Regulatory Research conducts a comprehensive research-and-standards program, which covers facility operation, engineering technology, accident evaluation, prediction of possible risks, plant location, health dangers, and waste management. The office aims at early identification of potential problems with reactors already in operation and constantly researches and monitors facilities for the disposal of nuclear waste.

This office first prepares a list of priorities among its problems to solve. It then seeks to research all possible ways to solve these problems. For example, to aid in the prevention of severe accidents, staff members probe the potential

A uranium-recovery facility in New Mexico. The Office of Nuclear Material Safety and Safeguards oversees the uranium-mining industry.

effects of various problems, such as the aging of reactor vessels (a vessel is a pressurized structure that houses the reactor core itself). From years of steady neutron irradiation (radiation bombardment), the kinds of steel and welds used in many of the older vessels become brittle. In an accident, such as a small-break loss-of-coolant accident in which one of the pipes carrying water to the reactor ruptures, a combination of intense heat buildup and high internal pressures (called "pressurized thermal shock") inside the vessel could pose a serious threat to older plants. Scientists conducting research at the Oak Ridge National Laboratory in Tennessee, the Naval Research Laboratory, and Materials Engineering Associates, Inc., developed a way to measure the steel's level of brittleness. As of 1985, utilities were not allowed to operate without NRC permission once their vessels had gone beyond a certain level of brittleness.

The Office of Nuclear Regulatory Research also examines steam generators, piping, and electrical and mechanical components to assure safe operation. In tests completed in 1985, researchers uncovered a potential problem with the material used to construct a particular O-ring that functions as a leak-preventing seal in a plant's coolant pump system. According to test results, the material used to manufacture the O-ring was not strong enough to endure the intense conditions of temperature, pressure, humidity, and radiation within the reactor. As a result, the pump supplier replaced the O-ring with one made of a stronger material.

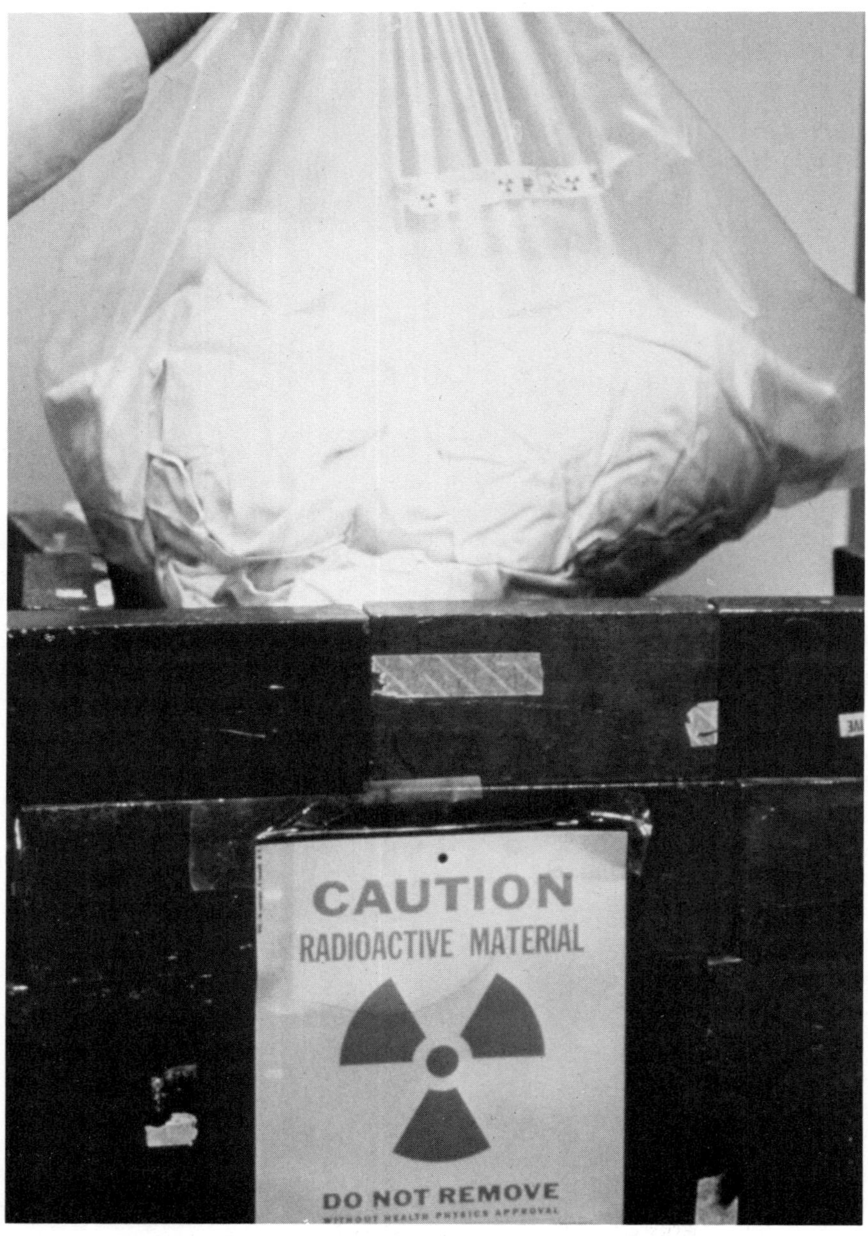

Nuclear medicine waste is placed in a receptacle for safe disposal. The NRC licenses nuclear material for use in medicine and regulates its disposal in low-level waste dumps.

FIVE

Beyond Nuclear Power Plant Licensing

The NRC works to ensure the safety of all United States nuclear facilities. However, as the 1979 accident at Three Mile Island demonstrated, accidents can happen despite precautions. To ensure swift reaction to such incidents and to other potential mishaps, the NRC has developed an incident response system. The agency also maintains a State Agreements Program, which allows for closer supervision by giving state governments greater command over the nuclear facilities within their borders. In addition, the NRC is responsible for regulating nuclear facilities other than power-generating plants; one such area is the burgeoning nuclear medicine industry, which has dramatically benefited the nation. Thus, in a variety of ways, the NRC touches the lives of many people who may only be aware of the agency's regulatory function.

Incident Response

Each year, a variety of accidents, malfunctions, and other potentially threatening incidents occur at the nation's more than 100 operating nuclear power plants. Many of these incidents are minor and are easily managed; others may require more supervision. To minimize the chance of mishap, the NRC Operations Center maintains 24-hour telephone hot lines to all of the nation's licensed reactors from its headquarters in Bethesda, Maryland. This is the

***Staff members at the NRC Operations Center in Bethesda, Maryland.
Under the NRC's 24-hour incident response program, these workers
receive the first report of an "event" at any licensed nuclear facility
in the United States.***

NRC's communications nerve center, where the first reports of incidents,
be they innocent or ominous, arrive. These incidents, also called "events,"
range from the excessive scram times experienced at the Monticello nuclear
generating plant in Monticello, Minnesota, in 1984 (in this case, a clogged filter
in the control-rod drive mechanism was causing the repeated tripping of
emergency shutoff systems) to a defective control circuit for an emergency
diesel generator (a backup system that provides power in the event that the
normal electricity used to run the plant fails) at the Rancho Seco nuclear power
generating station in Clay Station, California, in 1985. To help monitor
especially threatening situations, such as a 1986 fire at the Perry nuclear power
plant in northeastern Ohio, or to track menacing hurricanes such as hurricanes
Juan and Charley in 1986, the NRC calls in additional staff. In the Operations

Center all such events are screened and evaluated for their potential severity.

When a plant experiences a problem, the Operations Center must also determine whether it is a generic problem that may affect the safe operation of other facilities. If so, the NRC may issue a bulletin or "information notice" (a memo that rapidly provides important details but demands no specific action) to other licensees and construction-permit holders to whom the event may be relevant. Each plant must then decide on its own whether to take action to prevent a similar problem. In 1986, the NRC issued 112 such notices. For example, in March, after a reactor-coolant pump shaft (part of the reactor cooling system) failed at the Crystal River nuclear power plant in Red Level, Florida, the NRC sent an information notice to all power-reactor facilities with an operating license or construction permit. Other information notices in 1985 and 1986 concerned the potential failure of emergency diesel generators, stuck control rods (which normally regulate the amount of power produced in a reactor), problems in control-room emergency ventilation systems, and the reliability of safety valves.

When action is needed, the NRC's local regional office takes charge of the situation. In a major event that could threaten public safety, the regional office staff first forms a "base team" to represent the NRC and monitor the utility's performance. If a visit to the site becomes necessary, the office dispatches a "site team" to coordinate the NRC's response to the problem.

Although the regional offices remain on guard to help avert mishap, quick action on the part of the plant operators themselves can prevent many potential disasters. In the early morning hours of June 9, 1985, one of the two main water pumps tripped at the Davis-Besse nuclear power station in Oak Harbor, Ohio, depriving two steam generators of needed water for about 12 minutes. Before more water could be pumped to remedy the situation, the steam generators had nearly boiled dry—a potentially hazardous condition. By the time the NRC Operations Center in Bethesda learned of the event, 36 minutes later, the reactor had been brought to a successful shutdown and the plant was in stable, safe condition. NRC specialists later arrived to investigate the problem.

State Agreements Program

Because national concern about nuclear safety has risen dramatically, especially following the 1979 accident at Three Mile Island, 28 states have forged formal agreements with the NRC under which they assume certain regulatory responsibilities at nonpower nuclear facilities within their borders.

The State Agreements Program has allowed states to gain independent knowledge and understanding of nuclear risks and to take steps to prevent nuclear accidents. Through the program, state leaders are able to keep routinely informed of conditions at facilities located in their states.

The NRC periodically reviews Agreement States' radiation-control programs to confirm that they are adequate to protect the public. During such reviews, NRC technical staff accompany state inspectors to state-licensed facilities to evaluate inspector performance, to review the details of licensing, and to discern how well the facilities are complying with regulations. In addition, the NRC supplies Agreement States with expert technical aid. In 1985, for instance, the NRC gave assistance to a number of states. Tennessee received help evaluating an application for the use of tritium (a radioactive isotope of hydrogen) at a proposed Isotope Application Technology facility at Oak Ridge; the NRC helped Florida evaluate an application for a proposed computerized nuclear cardiology facility to aid in the study of heart disease; and the agency aided New York State health authorities in their evaluation of americium-241 contamination in a landfill and sewage-treatment incinerator.

Three technicians prepare nuclear fuel pellets at a processing plant. Under the NRC's State Agreements Program, individual states are able to monitor conditions at nuclear facilities within their borders, such as this one in Los Alamos, New Mexico.

*A dummy is "checked" for radioactive contamination after a simu-
lated accident, part of an NRC-sponsored course in health physics for
state employees. The NRC provides such training courses for partici-
pants in its State Agreements Program.*

The NRC also sponsors training courses to hone state workers' technical
and administrative skills. In 1986, for instance, the agency sponsored 12
short-term training courses, attended by some 224 state personnel. These
courses included health physics, industrial-radiography (X-ray photography)
safety, nuclear medicine procedures, uranium-mill inspection, transportation of
low-level radioactive waste and other nuclear materials, and on-the-job training
in licensing regulations.

The NRC also provides technical assistance to states wrestling with the
problems of low-level waste regulation and disposal. This task often takes the

form of helping in evaluation of license renewals for low-level waste-disposal sites. In 1986, the NRC provided help to Florida officials in the renewal of a waste-processor license and to Arizona in evaluating a disposal facility for nuclear waste generated by research at the University of Arizona.

Another area in which the NRC offers its expertise is in the regulation of uranium milling. When called upon, the agency will advise on matters including fulfillment of Environmental Protection Agency (EPA) requirements concerning safe levels of groundwater contamination and provide direct technical aid to states as needed. For example, in March 1986 the governor of New Mexico requested that the NRC take charge of uranium milling and mill tailings in the state because severe budget restraints had made state officials unable to comply with EPA regulations. The NRC did so.

A number of states have taken steps to become more directly involved in the regulation of nuclear power reactor operations and in other basic nuclear issues. Since 1980, for instance, Oregon has had a state resident inspector, authorized by state law, at the state's only nuclear power plant, the Trojan nuclear plant Unit 1 in Prescott. And Illinois officials perform periodic

Technicians demonstrate waste-disposal procedures at a below-ground radioactive-waste disposal facility in New Mexico. The NRC assists individual states in evaluating the safety of such sites.

A rail car carrying a spent-fuel shipping cask is deliberately crashed into a concrete wall at 81 miles per hour. Test demonstrations such as this one help to determine the safety of containers used to transport radioactive wastes.

inspections of low-level waste packaging and transport at NRC-licensed facilities, including reactors.

Agreement States may also participate in workshops that are specially planned for their benefit. In July and August of 1985, 275 state officials, representatives of localities, and representatives of American Indian tribes participated in a three-day seminar on the regulatory roles of the NRC and the federal Department of Transportation concerning spent-fuel transportation. The seminar's topics included shipping and inspection, emergency response, transportation requirements, and routing. Routing topics included route selection, strategies for reducing risks and accidents, and coordination among states. An emergency-preparedness discussion group focused on effective planning, procedures, training, and equipment and featured a half-day tour of the General Electric Company's spent-fuel storage facilities at Morris, Illinois. This tour included exhibits of the IF-300 rail-shipping cask (used for transporting radioactive materials), radiological monitoring vans, the Illinois state police hazardous-materials highway patrol car, and other escort vehicles. A one-day seminar held in Washington, D.C., in 1986 focused on the issues lawmakers must understand in order to enact responsible legislation regarding low-level waste disposal, transportation of radioactive materials, and other related issues.

In accordance with the Nuclear Waste Policy Act of 1982, which provided for federal consultation and cooperation with American Indian tribes as well as with states who may be affected by waste disposal, the NRC has met regularly with tribal representatives. In 1986, NRC staff attended several meetings held by the National Congress of American Indians, an organization that represents more than 200 tribes. The meetings addressed issues such as nuclear waste regulation, notification of transportation of high-level radioactive waste, training of transportation workers, and emergency preparedness.

Medical Licensing

Not all of the NRC's licensing activity involves power plants. To a lesser extent, the NRC also licenses materials for use in medicine. Each year in the United States, doctors and hospital technicians perform an estimated 7 million clinical procedures using radioactive materials, primarily to treat or diagnose disease.

Radioisotopes are used in nuclear medicine to perform diagnostic tests. For the most part, the techniques employ small amounts of radioactive material with blood samples or other patient specimens. On the basis of these extremely sensitive tests, medical specialists can, for example, determine vitamin B-12 levels or measure drug toxicity. In the mid-1980s, this kind of test constituted the majority of radioisotope studies in nuclear medicine.

Radiation therapy—the controlled use of radiation to treat life-threatening disease—is another major medical use of radioisotopes. Cancers, blood disorders, and hyperthyroidism (a thyroid-gland disorder that can be fatal if not treated) are often treated using radioactive drugs taken orally. In a treatment known as brachytherapy, a small amount of radioactive material such as the radioactive form of the chemical element cobalt may be sealed into a capsule and positioned on or in a patient's body to treat cancer while shielding healthy tissue from the radiation's effects. "Teletherapy" also uses sealed sources, usually cobalt-60, a radioactive isotope of cobalt, or cesium-137, a radioactive isotope of cesium. Contained in a special unit, these materials can produce

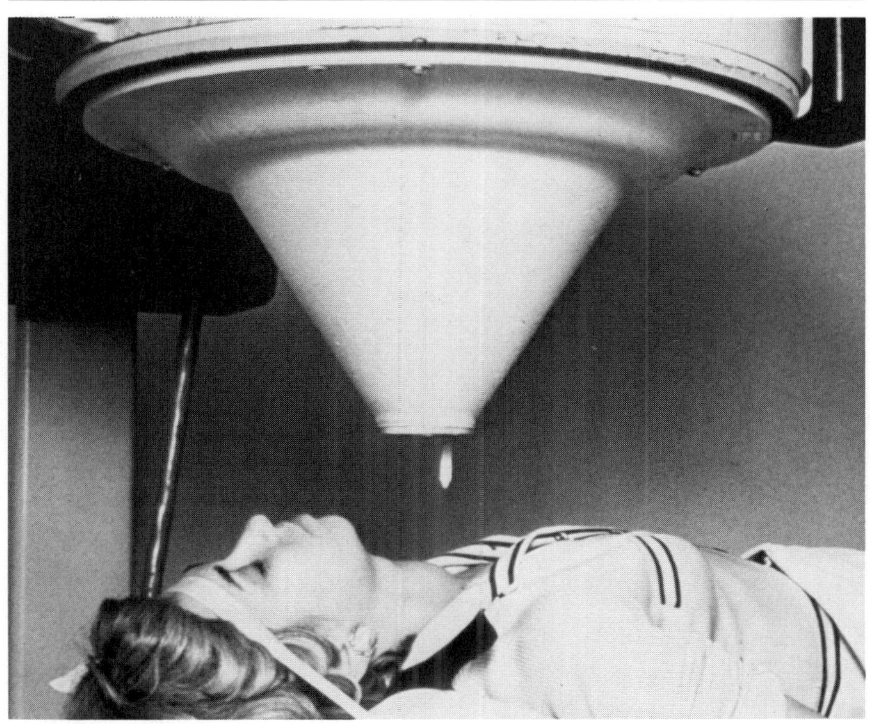

A patient undergoes a nuclear scanning procedure for treatment of a thyroid disorder. Nuclear materials are invaluable in detecting and treating disease.

intense radiation fields that technicians can selectively aim at a patient's cancerous tissue from a distance. Periodically, used cobalt is returned to research reactors to be recharged, after which it is taken back to hospitals.

Other diagnostic studies involve the injection of radioisotopes directly into a patient's body. Through the use of computers and special cameras that can photograph the radioactive substance as it moves within the body, specialists can create a scan of a patient's internal organ, for example, or a sophisticated analysis of the heart under stress.

Like reactor waste, the radioactive waste material generated by medical technology is subject to many disposal regulations. Some of this waste consists of the same elements produced by power reactors. Cesium-137 and cobalt-60, for example, both commonly used in nuclear medicine, can also be found in the cooling water that circulates around a reactor's core. Medical waste accounts for approximately seven percent of the low-level waste buried in radioactive-

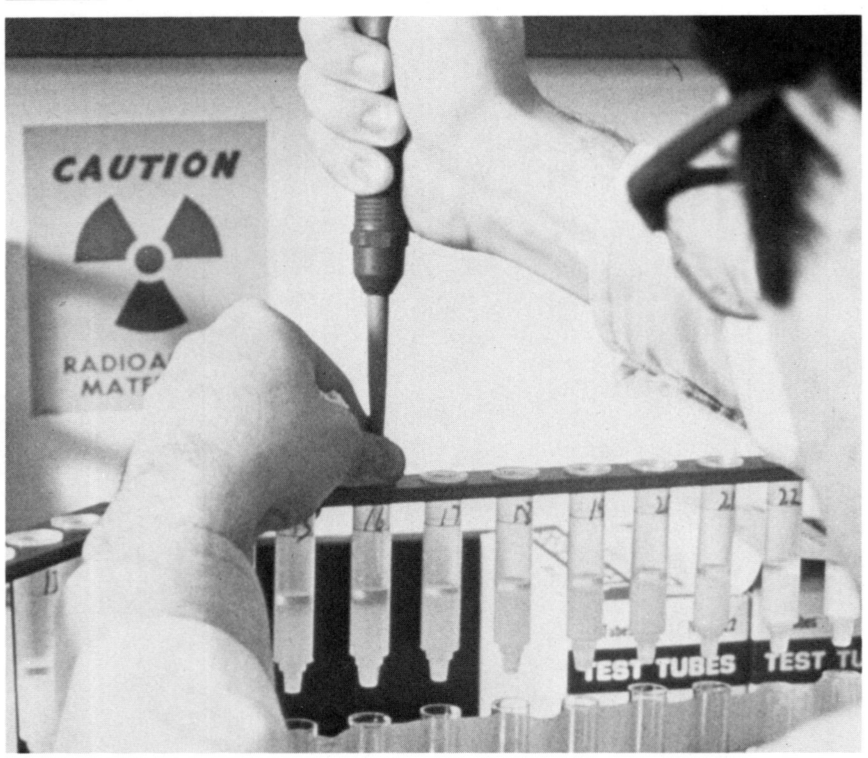

A lab technician adds radioactive chemicals to a patient's body fluids to test for abnormalities. The NRC licenses the use of nuclear materials in such medical procedures.

waste disposal sites. By comparison, reactor waste accounts for about 54 percent, according to figures from the Sierra Club, an environmental safety organization. However, medical waste accounts for less than one percent of the total number of curies (measures of radioactivity) dumped at waste sites. (The term *curie* comes from Marie and Pierre Curie, known for their pioneering work on radioactivity.) And although some reactor waste may remain radioactive for thousands of years, about three-quarters of the radioactive substances found in medical waste shipped to burial sites have a half-life of less than one week. (A half-life is the period required for half of a radioactive substance to disintegrate. For example, a one-week half-life means half of the substance will disintegrate after one week. After the second week, half of that remains—one-quarter of the original. After the third week, half of that remains, or one-eighth of the original.) Technetium-99m, with a half-life of

6 hours, accounts for some 60 percent of medical radioactive wastes shipped to burial sites. (The *m* stands for metastable, as opposed to technetium-99 without the *m*, a different radioactive material with a half-life of some 210,000 years.) Iodine-131, the other significant element of radioactive medical waste, has a half-life of eight days.

A cooling tower at a nuclear power plant symbolizes the looming menace that many see in nuclear energy. Through its efforts to ensure the safe operation of America's nuclear facilities, the NRC hopes to dispel such fears.

SIX

The NRC Tomorrow

Perhaps understandably, the NRC to many is guilty by association with nuclear power—a technology viewed as a menace to life and a threat to society. To others, however, nuclear energy is the power source of the future, a lifeblood that will be with us years after the world's supplies of oil, natural gas, and coal have been depleted. Very likely, the actual role of nuclear power tomorrow will be found somewhere between these extremes. But one thing is certain: Whatever the place of nuclear power in humanity's future, the NRC will help get it there.

In its relatively short lifetime, the NRC has guided U.S. nuclear policy toward ever-safer standards. Legislation has helped provide safer disposal of nuclear waste and proper handling of tailings from uranium mills. As new power plants are built, they will use newer and safer steels, welds, and safety precautions. And as the nuclear power industry evolves, the NRC will be part of that evolution.

For much of the public, this evolutionary process will go unnoticed. As dramatic as new safety devices may be, it is likely such positive advances will not counter the negative attention focused on a nuclear accident. For this reason, the nuclear power industry, and with it the NRC, will probably have to contend for years with an ongoing public perception of nuclear power as a safety and health hazard. Because they are beyond the technological grasp of most people, even the dramatic advances in nuclear medicine or research in biology and chemistry may not be able to alter the anxious relationship many Americans share with the atom.

As the nuclear power industry matures, some familiar tensions facing the NRC promise to remain. Further development of the nuclear industry is bound to continue to clash with questions about public safety and environmental health, even over seemingly minor problems. As the Union of Concerned Scientists pointed out in the book *Safety Second*, even small deficiencies can result in large accidents. On March 22, 1975, for example—shortly after the NRC came into existence—a worker using a candle to check for air leaks inside the Browns Ferry nuclear power plant in Decatur, Alabama, set electrical cable insulation, made of polyurethane, ablaze. The fire burned for more than seven hours under the main control room, destroying hundreds of cables—including those used to monitor the status of the reactors and to control safety devices. Employees were eventually able to bring the reactor under control using undamaged pieces of equipment that were not part of the plant's elaborate safety apparatus.

According to *Safety Second*, "Engineers of the Tennessee Valley Authority, operator of Browns Ferry, stated privately that a potentially catastrophic

In reaction to the Three Mile Island accident, several hundred anti-nuclear demonstrators hold a "die in" in San Francisco in 1979. Protest has accompanied the development of the nuclear industry since its beginnings.

In the wake of Three Mile Island, an antinuclear protester asks a pointed question.

radiation release was avoided 'by sheer luck.' " However, 12 days after the fire the NRC issued a directive to all nuclear power plant operators ordering them to review procedures for shutting down reactors. In addition, license holders were told to review and, if necessary, to revise procedures for use of combustible materials and ignition sources. More fire extinguishers were provided, fire hoses installed, and hydrants added. In 1981, "The Fire Protection Program for Nuclear Power Facilities Operating Prior to January 1, 1979," an NRC rule governing technical fire-protection specifications, took effect.

Looming over most conflicts between public safety concerns and the need for nuclear power is the specter of nuclear disaster. Among other things, Three Mile Island proved that a disaster can happen in the United States despite safety precautions. The Chernobyl accident proved that one nuclear accident can have severe worldwide repercussions. Yet in learning from past mistakes, the nuclear industry progresses to a higher awareness of public and environmental safety and health. As that trend continues, the NRC will without doubt enhance its role as guardian of those national resources.

U.S. Nuclear Regulatory Commission

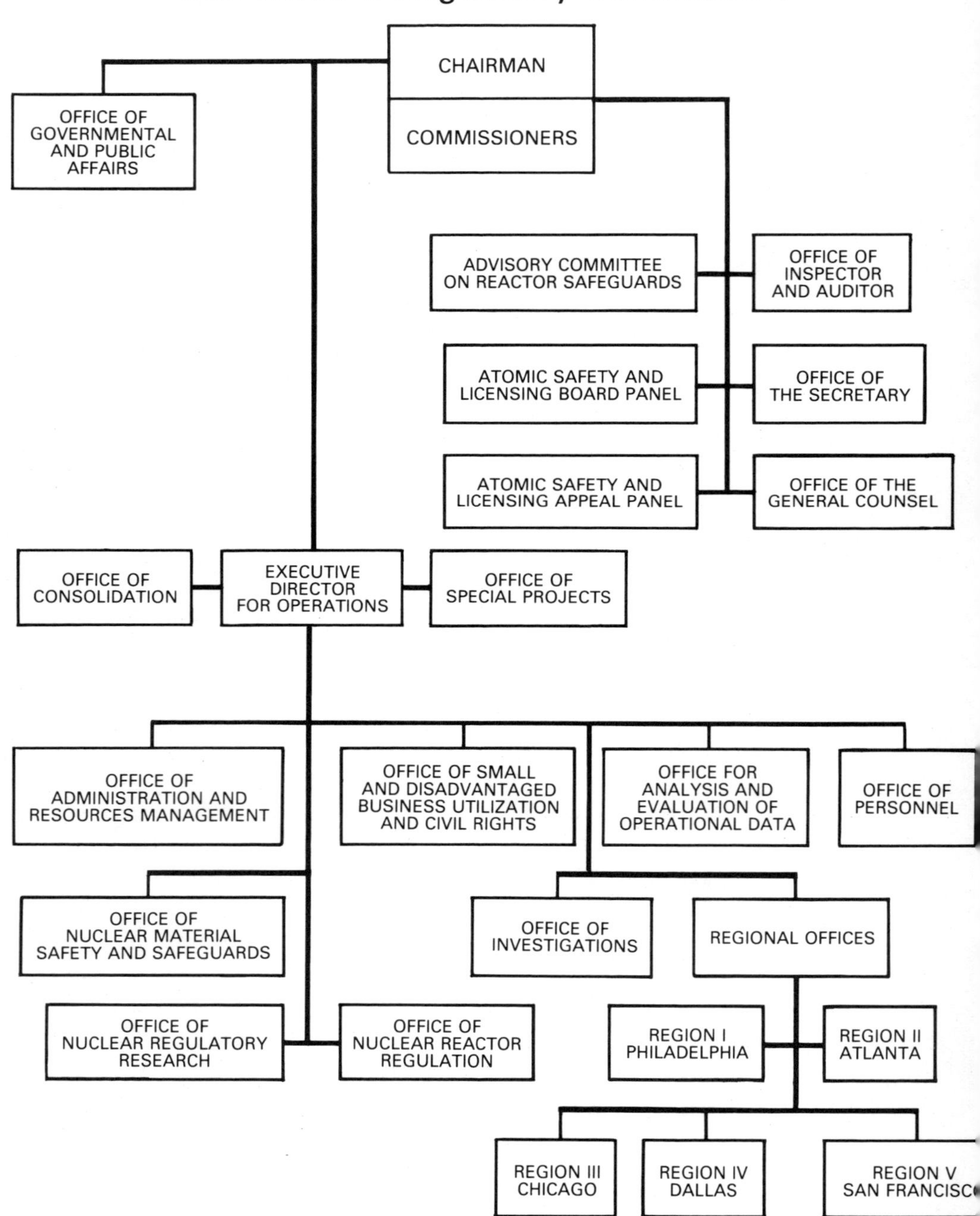

GLOSSARY

Boiling water reactor One of two main types of reactor operating in the United States. Fuel in a reactor's core heats water to steam, which drives a turbine to produce electricity. The used steam is cooled (condensed), recycled through the core again as water, reheated to steam to drive the turbine, then recooled and reheated over and over.

Containment building The steel-reinforced cement structure housing the nuclear reactor; designed to prevent escape of radioactivity through leaks or other accidents.

Control rod Made of a neutron-absorbing material, control rods are used to regulate the progress of nuclear fission in a reactor. When the rods are inserted into the reactor core, they absorb neutrons emitted during fission, rendering the neutrons incapable of splitting apart other fissionable atoms and thus slowing the nuclear reaction. To generate more heat, the control rods are withdrawn from the core, allowing more fission to occur.

Core The central part of a nuclear reactor, where controlled nuclear reactions occur and heat is produced.

Curie A measure of the amount of activity in a sample of radioactive material, equivalent to 37 billion emissions (disintegrations) per second. One gram (about 1/28 of an ounce) of natural uranium has an activity of about one-thousandth of a curie.

Fission The process that goes on inside a nuclear reactor. When a neutron, a subatomic particle, strikes another atom's nucleus, it splits the nucleus into two or more lighter parts. As an atom's heavy nucleus is split into fragments, the process—fission—releases a large amount of energy, primarily heat, and also more neutrons, which shoot away at high speed, striking other atoms and causing them to split apart in a chain reaction.

Fossil fuels Fuels, such as coal, natural gas, and oil, that are formed in the earth from plant or animal remains and are therefore limited resources.

Fuel rod A tube filled with uranium or plutonium fuel. Bundles of these tubes, protected inside metal capsules, are loaded into the reactor core.

Half-life   The amount of time required for a radioactive substance to lose half of its radioactivity.

Meltdown   The most severe accident that can occur at a nuclear power plant, when the reactor cooling system fails and fuel rods melt. In the worst kind of meltdown, the reactor core could burn, or melt, through the ground below the power station and release highly dangerous radiation.

Pressurized water reactor   Along with the boiling water reactor, one of the two main types of nuclear reactor operating in the United States. Water circulating through a reactor's core is kept at high pressure, preventing it from boiling. This superheated water is used as a heating element to turn "regular" water into steam, which drives a turbine to produce electricity. The steam is condensed into water again, then reheated into steam in a cyclic process.

Radiation   Energetic subatomic particles such as neutrons, alpha, and beta particles that, ejected by unstable elements (for example, uranium, plutonium, and radium), travel at extremely high speeds, creating streams or rays of particles that can be harnessed as energy but can also be very harmful.

Radioactivity   The spontaneous change of one kind of atom into another by emission of radiation; often measured in curies.

Reactor   The nuclear reactor core and its immediate container.

Reactor vessel   The steel tank containing the reactor core.

Rem (roentgen equivalent man)   The standard unit of measure of biological damage from radiation exposure.

Scram   Emergency shutdown of a nuclear reactor.

Thermal pollution   The discharge of heated liquid, such as waste water from a nuclear power plant, into lakes, rivers, or streams at a temperature harmful to these environments.

SELECTED REFERENCES

Allardice, Corbin, and Edward R. Trapnell. *The Atomic Energy Commission.* New York: Praeger, 1974.

Cook, Constance Ewing. *Nuclear Power and Legal Advocacy.* Lexington, MA: Heath, 1980.

Del Sesto, Steven L. *Science, Politics, and Controversy: Civilian Nuclear Power in the United States, 1946–74.* Boulder, CO: Westview Press, 1979.

Energy Information Administration, Office of Coal, Nuclear, Electric and Alternate Fuels. *Commercial Nuclear Power: Prospects for the United States and the World.* Washington, D.C.: U.S. Government Printing Office, 1986.

Gofman, John W., and Arthur R. Tamplin. *Poisoned Power: The Case Against Nuclear Power Plants.* Emmaus, PA: Rodale Press, 1971.

Goode, Stephen. *The Nuclear Energy Controversy.* New York: Watts, 1980.

Halacy, Dan. *Nuclear Energy.* New York: Watts, 1978.

Hawkea, Nigel. *Chernobyl: The End of the Nuclear Dream.* New York: Random House, 1986.

Hewlett, Richard G., and Oscar E. Anderson, Jr. *The New World 1939–46: A History of the United States Atomic Energy Commission.* University Park: Pennsylvania State University Press, 1962.

Hoyle, Fred. *Energy or Extinction? The Case for Nuclear Energy.* New York: Heinemann Educational Books Ltd., 1977.

Lilienthal, David E. *Change, Hope and the Bomb.* Princeton, NJ: Princeton University Press, 1963.

Mazuzan, George T., and Samuel Walker. *Controlling the Atom: The Beginnings of Nuclear Regulation, 1946–62.* Berkeley: University of California Press, 1985.

Nader, Ralph, and John Abbotts. *The Menace of Atomic Energy*. New York: Norton, 1977.

Ott, Karl O., and Bernard I. Spinrad, eds. *Nuclear Energy: A Sensible Alternative*. New York: Plenum Press, 1985.

Rolph, Elizabeth S. *Nuclear Power and the Public Safety*. Lexington, MA: Heath, 1979.

Stephens, Mark. *Three Mile Island*. New York: Random House, 1980.

Union of Concerned Scientists. *Safety Second: The NRC and America's Nuclear Power Plants*. Bloomington: Indiana University Press, 1987.

INDEX

Advisory Committee on Reactor
  Safeguards, 42, 57
Alvin W. Vogtle, Jr., nuclear
  power plant, 70, 71, 72
American Chemical Society, 37
American Indians, 83, 84
Americium, 68, 80
Antinuclear groups, 32, 33, 36
Atomic bomb, 17, 19, 21, 25,
  30, 63
Atomic energy. *See* Nuclear
  energy
Atomic Energy Act of 1946, 21,
  25, 28
Atomic Energy Act of 1954, 28
Atomic Energy Commission
  (AEC), 16, 17, 21, 22, 23, 25,
  28, 30–39
Atomic Safety and Licensing
  Appeal Panel, 57, 58
Atomic Safety and Licensing
  Board Panel, 42, 57, 58, 70
"Atoms for Peace" speech (Ei-
  senhower), 27–28

Bethesda, Maryland, 65, 77, 79
Browns Ferry nuclear power
  plant, 90

Calvert Cliffs nuclear power
  plant, 33, 36, 66
Cancer, 15, 32, 33, 37, 41, 46,
  84, 85
Carter, Jimmy, 50, 52
Cesium, 84, 85
Change, Hope and the Bomb
  (Lilienthal), 22
Chemical Technology, 37
Chernobyl nuclear power plant,
  17, 52–55, 61, 91
"China Syndrome," 32
Cobalt, 84, 85

Comanche Peak nuclear power
  plant, 65, 70
Congress, U.S., 16, 21, 23, 28,
  33, 46, 52, 57, 59
Crystal River nuclear power
  plant, 79
Curie, Marie and Pierre, 86

Daily Progress, 37
Davis-Besse nuclear power
  plant, 79
Dean, Gordon, 25, 27, 28
Diablo Canyon nuclear power
  plant, 61, 70
Docking, Robert, 36
Dole, Hollis, 35

Eisenhower, Dwight D., 27, 28
Emergency core-cooling system
  (ECCS), 32, 33, 37, 63
Energy, Department of, 43, 73
Energy Reorganization Act of
  1974, 39, 69
Energy Research and Develop-
  ment Administration, 16, 39
Enrico Fermi nuclear power
  plant, 37
Environmental protection, 31,
  33, 36, 70–72, 90
Environmental Protection
  Agency (EPA), 45, 82

Federal Bureau of Investigation
  (FBI), 66, 68
Fission, 25, 27, 62
Ford, Gerald, 41
Fossil fuels, 31, 89
Friends of the Earth, 36
Fusion, 27

General Accounting Office, 33,
  35, 47

General Electric Company, 28,
  31, 69, 83
Gofman, John W., 31, 32
Gravel, Mike, 36, 37, 38

Half-life, 86, 87
Hambleton, William H., 35
Harrisburg, Pennsylvania, 47,
  49
Hiroshima, Japan, 19, 21

Interior, Department of the, 35
International Atomic Energy
  Agency, 55
Iodine, 87

Justice, Department of, 59, 61

Kansas Geological Survey, 35
Kemeny, John G., 50
Kemeny Commission, 50, 52,
  55
Kiev, Soviet Union, 52

Lilienthal, David E., 22, 25
Low-level Radioactive Waste
  Policy Act of 1980, 52
Luberoff, B. J., 37

McMillan, Edwin M., 30
Maintenance and Surveillance
  Program Plan, 72
Manhattan Project, 21, 22, 30
Materials Engineering Associ-
  ates, Inc., 75
Monticello nuclear power plant,
  78

Nader, Ralph, 36, 37
Nagasaki, Japan, 19, 21
National Environmental Policy
  Act of 1969, 33, 34, 36
Nixon, Richard, 36
Nuclear accidents, 17, 23, 32,
  33, 47, 49, 50, 52–55, 57, 75,
  77, 80

Nuclear energy
  dangers of, 16, 17, 31, 33, 37,
    46, 49, 52, 55, 70–72, 79, 91
  used for peaceful purposes, 21,
    25, 27, 28
  research and development, 16,
    22, 41
  used in warfare, 17, 19, 22,
    27. *See also* Nuclear power
    plants
Nuclear fuels, 22, 31, 46, 52.
  See also Uranium
Nuclear medicine, 84–87, 90
Nuclear power plants, 15, 17,
  23, 28, 31, 33, 37, 38, 41, 42,
  67, 69, 70, 79, 82, 84
Nuclear reactors, 23, 25, 30, 31,
  32, 33, 37, 41, 42, 43, 45, 46,
  47, 49, 52, 57, 62–63, 69, 70,
  79, 83, 85, 90, 91
Nuclear Regulatory Commission (NRC)
  establishment of, 16, 41
  operations, 64–69
  power-plant licensing, 41–43,
    57–58, 80, 81
  program offices, 69–75
  regional offices, 64, 69, 79
  responsibilities of, 17, 19
  safety standards, 57, 89
  structure of, 57–75
Nuclear waste, 17, 33, 35, 37,
  44, 45, 46, 52, 72, 81, 82, 83,
  84, 85, 86, 87, 89
Nuclear Waste Policy Act of
  1982, 84
Nuclear weapons, 22, 27, 30

Office of Administration and
  Resources Management, 64,
  65
Office for Analysis and Evalua-
  tion of Operational Data, 64,
  66
Office of Consolidation, 64, 65
Office of the General Counsel, 59

Office of Governmental and
Public Affairs, 59, 61
Office of Inspection and
Enforcement, 50, 72
Office of Inspector and Auditor,
59, 61, 66
Office of International
Programs, 61
Office of Investigations, 64, 66
Office of Nuclear Material
Safety and Safeguards, 69,
72, 73
Office of Nuclear Reactor Regu-
lation, 69
Office of Nuclear Regulatory
Research, 69, 70, 72, 73, 75
Office of Personnel, 64, 68
Office of the Secretary, 59
Office of Small and Disadvan-
taged Business Utilization
and Civil Rights, 64, 66
Office of Special Projects, 64, 65
Office of State Programs, 61
Oil shortage, 37, 38, 43
Oppenheimer, J. Robert, 17
Organization of Petroleum Ex-
porting Countries (OPEC),
37–38, 43
Oyster Creek nuclear power
plant, 31

Perry nuclear power plant, 78
Plutonium, 30, 52

Radiation therapy, 84
Radioactive waste. *See* Nuclear
waste
Radioisotopes, 31, 61, 72, 84, 85
Rancho Seco nuclear power
plant, 78
Rowe nuclear power plant, 28

Safety Second, 90
Schlesinger, James R., 36
Scientists' Institute for Public
Information, 37

Scrams, 66, 78
Seaborg, Glenn T., 30, 31, 36
Senate, U.S., 22, 37, 57
Shippingport nuclear power
plant, 28, 37, 70
Skubitz, Joe, 35
Soviet Union, 52, 53, 55
State Agreements Program, 61,
77, 79–84

Tamplin, Arthur R., 31, 32
Technetium, 86, 87
Tennessee Valley Authority,
22, 65
Thermal pollution, 31, 33
Thermonuclear bomb, 27
Thornburg, Richard L., 49
Three Mile Island nuclear
power plant, 17, 47, 49, 50,
55, 61, 65, 72, 73, 77, 79, 91
Transportation, Department of,
73, 83
Tritium, 80
Trojan nuclear power plant, 82
Truman, Harry S., 21

Union of Concerned Scientists,
37, 46–47, 90
United Nations, 27
Uranium, 22, 46, 47, 52, 73, 82,
89
Uranium Mill Tailings Radia-
tion Control Act of 1978, 46
Uranium Recovery Field Office,
73
U.S. Army, 19, 21
U.S. Geological Survey, 70

Vienna, Austria, 55, 61

Water Quality Improvement
Act of 1970, 33, 36
Westinghouse, 28, 69
World War II, 19, 21, 22, 25, 30
Wright, Judge James Skelly,
33, 34

Yeltsin, Boris N., 53

Fred Clement, a free-lance writer, holds a degree in English from Princeton University. He has previously worked as a reporter and editor and has won several Pennsylvania journalism awards, including a 1979 Keystone Press Award for the best news story and, in 1984, the Jesse H. Neal Editorial Achievement Award. He is the author of *The Department of the Interior,* another volume in the KNOW YOUR GOVERNMENT series published by Chelsea House.

Arthur M. Schlesinger, jr., served in the White House as special assistant to Presidents Kennedy and Johnson. He is the author of numerous acclaimed works in American history and has twice been awarded the Pulitzer Prize. He taught history at Harvard College for many years and is currently Albert Schweitzer Professor of the Humanities at the City College of New York.

PICTURE CREDITS:

American College of Nuclear Physicians: pp. 16, 76, 85, 86; AP/Wide World Photos: pp. 40, 47, 48, 49, 53, 78; Atlantic Richfield Co.: p. 38; Department of Energy: pp. 2, 20, 25, 44, 45, 51, 65, 67, 71, 80, 82, 83, 88; Department of Energy/Energy Technology Visuals Collection: cover; Library of Congress: p. 24; National Archives: pp. 14, 18, 22, 23, 26, 29, 32, 34, 35, 36; Nuclear Regulatory Commission: pp. 30, 46, 58, 60, 68; Public Citizen: pp. 74, 81; Reuters/Bettmann Newsphotos: p. 54; UPI/Bettmann Newsphotos: pp. 27, 50, 64, 90, 91; U.S. Council for Energy Awareness: pp. 43, 56, 62.

Clement, Fred

The Nuclear Regulatory Commission

353.0087   CLE   18814

DATE DUE	BORROWER'S NAME	ROOM NUMBER
DEC. 1		
MAY 2 1		
JUN 5		

<table>
<tr><th>DATE
DUE</th><th>BORROWER'S NAME</th><th>ROOM
NUMBER</th></tr>
</table>